# Smoke in the Mountains Cookbook

## The Art of Appalachian Barbecue

# Smoke in the Mountains Cookbook

## The Art of Appalachian Barbecue

Kent "The Deck Chef" Whitaker

QUAIL RIDGE PRESS

*Preserving America's Food Heritage*

**Library of Congress Cataloging-in-Publication Data**

Whitaker, Kent, 1965-
    Smoke in the mountains cookbook : the art of Appalachian barbecue / by Kent "The Deck Chef" Whitaker.
      p. cm.
      Includes index.
      ISBN 1-893062-61-9
    1. Barbecue cookery—Appalachian Region. I. Title.

      TX840.B3W46 2004
      641.5'784'0974—dc22                      2004010159

Front cover photo by Macee Whitaker.
Design by Cynthia Clark.
Printed in Canada.

**QUAIL RIDGE PRESS**
P. O. Box 123 • Brandon, MS 39043 • 1-800-343-1583
email: info@quailridge.com • www.quailridge.com

# Dedication

To my son Macee
who beat me once in a recipe contest.
He will never stop bragging on that one!

**GRILL MASTER JAKE SAYS —**
Let's get cookin'.

# Table of Contents

# Real Neat Eats

**In my travels all over the Appalachian region,** I always search out local barbecue restaurants.  Throughout the book you'll find pages containing profiles and photographs of my favorites, plus interesting stories about some of my barbecue buddies, and even some products highlighted that I consider to be barbecue standards.

# Preface

This book is about one of the subjects I love in life—barbecue and outdoor cooking! In the mid 1980s my wife and I discovered, on a college-married-couple budget, that frozen pot pies were pretty boring seven days a week. Between the two of us, Jamie was the cook. Back then all I knew about were pancakes, waffles and Pop-Tarts®; she knew about steaks, stews, veggies and chili! (I do still make great pancakes, by the way.)

One winter evening, the two of us went to a local grocery store in Murfreesboro, Tennessee, to stock up on frozen fish sticks, when we came across a small table-top grill marked down half price. We grabbed a few cheap steaks, the grill, and some charcoal, and headed home. In a freezing rain, we grilled out on the concrete walkway of our apartment complex. During the course of the winter we probably grilled out four days a week. We were hooked on outdoor cooking! You can imagine our excitement when we got a grill with a cover! Then a smoker. Now people call me **The Deck Chef** because I love to cook outside on the deck. And under the deck I have about seven grills, smokers and such stored until needed. Sometimes we end up cooking for about 40 people at a college football game. At the tender age of 11, my son Macee was knee-deep in his first chili cook-off and tailgate party during an NCAA championship football game.

Since college, I have traveled all over the South and the Appalachian region on vacations, business, and just for the heck of it. On every trip, I make a point to find the local best of the best barbecue or steak house. Sometimes I look for a good "meat and three." Wherever I end up, you can bet I find my way back to the pit master, the chef, or Aunt Betsy working the oven to get a few tips and tricks. The one thing that I have learned along the way is that people who do barbecue for a living—or for fun—take it very seriously. As my barbecue buddy Neva Owens said to me, "It's more than just cooking to me. It's an art form."

In this book I have passed along to you all my favorite recipes plus secrets, tips, and hints that I have learned along the way. I hope you enjoy them. Now get out, fire up some smoke and get cooking!

— *Kent "The Deck Chef" Whitaker*

# Special Thanks

To my mom and dad, Eli and Arleta. Somewhere along the way, their life lessons took hold. Thanks for not locking the fridge.

My older brothers, Ty and Scot, who always took care of their baby brother, except for a few stitches, bruises and such.

To Tonya, my brother Scot's wife, who cooks for a living, is a great source for information, and has great recipes and ideas. She also sees the inner chef in my son.

And, of course, to all of my nieces, Cailey, Colleen, Tyler, Torrey, and Emma Rose. And to my nephew, Ethan.

To "Grill Master" Jake. He listens to many bad jokes and rambles during overnight smoke sessions . . . but he knows he will always get a bite. Every deck chef should have a Golden Retriever.

To Jamie and her family, Jen and Jeremy.

To Wes, Kat, Ashton, and of course, Logan, who told me I was part of his family.

To Robin, who told me I could do this, often when others had better things to do.

To Linda and Homer Hickam. A very special thanks for helping keep my son's fire burning with these simple words, "Aim high!"

Also, to all of the people I have talked to and interviewed, and to those who let me wander about their kitchens and smoke houses. Thanks, Neva—Georgia's barbecue diva!

And a very special thanks to Sheila and everyone at Quail Ridge Press.

# Gettin' Fired Up

**It's not all barbecue, my friends.** Before you get started cooking outdoors, it's important to know what's what. Most people consider firing up the gas grill and lighting some charcoal for a few burgers as barbecuing. Because of the huge amount of discount department store grills sold every summer that have BARBECUE printed on the box, a blurred view of what barbecue is has occurred. Jamie and I were the same way during college. We bought a small grill and thought we were BARBECUE masters. It took a while to realize we needed some wood smoke to get the flavor we desired.

We will cover a few styles of outdoor cooking in this section with a heavy leaning towards barbecue. Definitions to common terms you may hear in the barbecuing world are also covered, as well as some stuff that just pops into my mind.

All terms, descriptions and definitions in this book come from years of standing in smoke while rain and snow poured over me. They also come from my friends, different restaurant pit masters and chefs. As you'll find out, there are very few set rules in barbecue. Most of them deal with internal meat temperatures. Almost everything else is up for discussion.

# Barbecue

Barbecue cooking means that you slow cook your food using low heat and lots of smoke. Usually coals, charcoal, wood chunks or a combination of all are used to produce a heat source with smoke. This is done for several

*These Boston Butts were rubbed with Kent's Basic Rub (page 67) before cooking. To make them as tender as possible, they were rubbed again, covered with Macee's Easy Sweet BBQ Sauce (page 41), and wrapped in foil for the last hour or so of the cooking process.*

hours in a covered smoker. The temperature often may never rise above 200 to 250 degrees. The important thing is the internal temperature of the food. By cooking low and slow with smoke, the meat takes on that trademark flavor.

Before we had freezers and refrigerators, people smoked meats as a way of preserving them. Often barbecue pit masters used sauces, marinades and rubs to enhance flavor. In the old days,

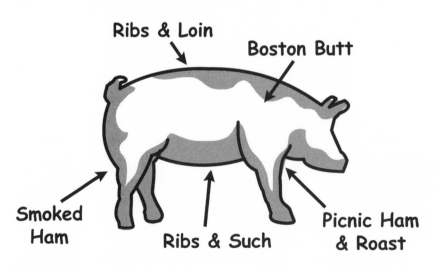

Ribs & Loin

Boston Butt

Smoked Ham

Ribs & Such

Picnic Ham & Roast

these sauces were often developed to help preserve the meat or cover up unpleasant flavors. After a while we started using sauces and refrigerators and such to enhance flavor instead of just covering it up.

## Grilling

Grilling is what most people do when they think they are barbecuing. Gas grills, charcoal grills, and tabletop grills are sold in the United States in incredible numbers. When you grill, you cook the food over direct high heat. The temperature can reach about 600 degrees and more! Grilling has been around for a long, long time. People grilled outdoors before the modern stove moved us inside. Grilling uses fuels such as gas, charcoal and wood.

Preparation is what makes for good grilling. With a bit of extra time, seasoning and basting, any meat cooked over a grill can produce fantastic flavors. There are several recipes in this book that will show you how to turn a simple burger or grilled chicken breast into a feast.

## Smoking & Indirect Cooking

This type of cooking is where the heat source is kept away from the food that is cooking— or smoking, to be exact. Often you will

*Morrison BBQ's smoker. (See page 234)*

find a smoke box or firebox as a completely separate chamber or piece on the smoker. Smoldering coals, wood and wood chunks are used to produce heat and smoke. (Wood chunks are smaller pieces of wood pre-packed and sold in many stores.) The heat and smoke pass from the lower smoke box into the cooking chamber. The smoke and low heat fill the chamber, surround the food, and then pass through another hole on the opposite side of the smoke box. This form of cooking takes a very long time. I know a guy who smokes meat for about a whole day! The great thing about smoking meat is that the flavor is unbeatable. The presentation of the finished product often has a darker outside and a pink inside. Again, this type of cooking is very close to slow barbecuing.

## SMOKE NOTE

Back in the colonial period of the United States, many pigs were set free to forage for food in the woods. When needed, they were hunted. Our colonial forefathers became very good at hosting feasts of outdoor cooking.

According to the book *Eating, Drinking and Visiting in the Old South* by Joe Gray Taylor, the average colonial southerner ate close to five pounds of pork compared to only one pound of beef annually. Heck, I ate almost five pounds of pork at a football tailgate party last season.

## Pit Cooking

This form of cooking has been around for a long time and variations of it can be found all over the world. During any given Saturday in college, the Ag fraternity would fire up a pit dug in the ground, and feed just about everybody in a 12-mile radius of the campus. In the South and other parts of the country, whole hogs are cooked over a fire-and-smoke-filled pit. The basic idea is that you dig a big hole, start a fire in it, smolder it, add your meat, cover it, go drink a beer or 20, and many hours later come back, dig it up and enjoy your dinner.

# Fryer

If you get a chance to eat a Cajun fried turkey, take advantage of it. Over the last few years, the propane deep fryer has really risen in popularity. Today's version includes a huge pot, fire stand, propane tank and more. During the fall you can often find outdoor deep fryers for sale in many stores. Just don't do it under the carport or in the house. Almost every deep-fried bird I have tried has been injected with some sort of seasoning.

# Broiling

Broiling is cooking with heat at very high temperatures. Often broiling is done with temperatures above 600 degrees. The meat is placed low over very hot coals and flame. The meat is basted often to prevent burning. Broiling is considered cooking with the heat coming from the top, as in a modern day oven. Broiling used to be considered cooking over high heat on a grill. This is also called searing.

# Searing

Searing is not burning! Searing means to quickly cook the meat at a high heat close to the flames or coals. This seals in flavor . . . like broiling in an oven.

*The crew at Owens Barbecue always has fun, whether it's behind the counter, out by the smokers, planning a menu, or even riding an antique bike.*

# Smokey's Hickory Smoke BBQ

**255 Holston Road • Wytheville, Virginia 24382**
**(276) 228-9014**

**800 E. Main Street • Wytheville, Virginia 24382**
**(276) 228-6622**

Ron Boone first started barbecuing in the mid 1980s. He entered a few competitions and then decided to make the big leap into the restaurant business. "It was a natural progression," Boone says. "I had decided to change jobs, and barbecuing was something that I

loved doing." The answer to his desire for an new career and his love for smoked meats turned into Smokey's Hickory Smoke BBQ

According to Ron, his restaurant is located "in the middle." Ron's wife Marsha said, "People from

Southwest Virginia, West Virginia, Tennessee and North Carolina often use Smokey's as a place to meet. It's easy to get to right off Interstate 81 at exit 71. People can come from all directions. We've been told that Smokey's is the best barbecue in Southwest Virginia." Ron enjoys getting involved in the community as well as cooking great 'que. You'll find Smokey's at local charity golf events, chamber of commerce fund-raisers, and more.

While you're there, ask Ron for his baked bean recipe. Good luck! Many people, including U.S. Senator Chuck Robb, have tried in vain to get Ron's recipe for baked beans.

**GREAT EATS:** The specialty of the house is the pork. But every Friday, Smokey's offers up huge helpings of St. Louis-style ribs. "They take a while, so we make a whole bunch and put them on our barbecue buffet," Boone told me.

**NEAT THING:** If you are ever in Wytheville for the annual Christmas parade, look for Ron, his crew and the bright yellow catering van pulling a huge smoker all decked out for the holidays. Even Santa has to eat!

# 'Que Know-How

**The stories are long . . . and longer.**  No one can pinpoint the day that barbecue was invented.  I have driven all around the South, and I have yet to find a roadside plaque that says barbecue was invented here in some year.

   According to several barbecue pit masters I have met, barbecuing is thought to have begun with some Caribbean Indians. Barbecue lore has it that they taught the Spanish sailors the art of BARBACOA, which I was told by a barbecue judge means something about cooking over wood and sticks.  The basic idea is that the Indians placed meat on green wooden sticks arranged over a fire.  (Heck, that's what we did in Cub Scouts!)  The flames under the green wood heated up the sticks and produced the smoky barbecue flavor we all love.  GET THE SLAW!

   You can separate barbecue in many ways—Carolina-style, Memphis-style, Kansas City-style, Texas-style and Southern-style barbecuing to name only a few.  As you move west across the Mississippi River, beef is often the preferred meat.  On the other side pork is often the choice.

   Pigs were all over the South at the turn of the century, the Civil War and before.  It was simple.  The terrain and climate made it perfect for farmers to raise pigs in the East and South. So when they needed something to cook, good old boys looked to the pig-pen for dinner. Carolina- and Southern-style barbecue incorporates foods and flavors from the Eastern Seaboard to the old South. Often the worst parts of meat found the way to the tables of poor Southerners. These people quickly discovered that marinating the meat, using spices, and cooking it at low temperatures made these tough chunks of meat not just edible but down right tasty. Often simple mustard and vinegar rubs were all that was needed.

A barbecue cookout was, and still is, a popular way for politicians to lobby for votes. Organizers of political rallies before and after the Civil War would provide barbecue, lemonade, and most likely a bit of hard cider. Political rallies like those made famous by Lincoln, Jackson and more are still carried on today.

Well, call us Southern-Appalachian-hillbilly-folk smart. We know a good thing when we see it . . . and eat it. After a few political rallies, many organizations such as churches picked up on the idea. Soon members of the congregation were bringing favorite family dishes to the church barbecue. Today we call it a covered dish dinner. People love to eat, and when you can get a bunch of folk together from different walks of life, feed them and make them happy, your message tends to come across better.

During the Civil War, pork was part of Southern national pride. Pigs were easy to raise, required little space, and could feed a hungry army. Pork was often the main dish at political rallies. Barbecue dinners were a great way to raise funds for the war and raise morale.

According to mountain barbecue folklore, the pits that served the political and church barbecues soon became permanent structures. Often after a big event, the pit master would continue to cook up a few extra pounds of meat for sale. Pretty soon small structures made of wood and tin covered the cooking areas, and after a week of work in the fields, the local pit master would open the pit for weekend business.

IMAGE USED WITH PERMISSION FROM CHICKAMAUGA-CHATTANOOGA NATIONAL MILITARY PARK.

*Over 15,000 veterans and dignitaries presented this invitation to the Chattanooga Barbecue which was held in 1889 to promote the idea for a national military park. Veterans from both the Union and Confederate armies led the drive to form a memorial to the battle fought there. On August 19, 1890, an act was signed to establish the Chickamauga-Chattanooga National Military Park.*

# Asheville Mennonite Church

### 49 Bull Mountain Road • Asheville, North Carolina 28805
### (828) 298-4487

**D**uring a road trip in search of great barbecue, I pulled into a parking lot somewhere in Asheville, North Carolina, to check my trusted Atlas. When I looked up again to read a street sign, I saw a small yellow sign advertising the Annual Smoked Chicken Lunch.

Of course I had to follow these small signs to their source.

They led me to a small church nestled in a hillside with eight huge smokers going full blast. Everywhere people were laughing and eating. Kids were running and playing, and a nice lady walked past me with two pies and a bag full of chicken. What a barbecue find!

The Asheville Mennonite Church hosts their Annual Smoked Chicken Lunch to raise money. "We've done everything you can think of to raise money to send our kids to a youth convention," Pastor Pat McFarren said. "They were all so much work and took so much time, that we came up with the chicken idea." The first feast was about 1993 and it has grown every year.

According to volunteer smoke master Wendell Kurtz, the food for the event is cooked in two sessions with over 490 seasoned, smoked chicken halves cooked each time. That's a bunch of smoked chicken! "The secret to our chicken is the Cajun-style seasoning and the slow smoke time. We cook them for over eight hours," Wendell said.

I ate my fill of Wendell's chicken and a nice slice of cake before leaving the hospitality of the Asheville Mennonite Church. If you want to find out when the next event is, feel free to call the church.

Before you knew it, barbecue restaurants had popped up all over the place. People were driving cars on weekend get-a-ways, and buying prepackaged foods at big grocery stores. The small covered pit had evolved into small businesses across the country.

Today you can still find a good church barbecue or political rally serving up some pork platters around the Appalachian Mountains. Check out the profile on my friends in Asheville, North Carolina, at the Asheville Mennonite Church (opposite page).

Simply put, barbecue is the fine craft of cooking food outdoors using low or indirect heat for long periods of time. This unique method of cooking has evolved from region to region using the meats, smokers, woods and spices available in each area. The neat thing is all of the methods of outdoor cooking have lots of things in common, and all provide a finished product with a rich and distinct flavor that you just can't get cooking indoors.

To help you achieve the same success, I have included tips from the pit masters, some important information about handling your food safely, and a section on selecting the best wood. Get the fire goin' . . . let's eat!

# Tips from the Pit Masters

**The best way to learn how to make great barbecue** is to just start making it. Ask questions and try again. The great thing about this is you get to eat and cook all of the time. When I talk with owners of barbecue restaurants and pit masters, I always ask for tips. Here are a few of the most common tips from some of the South's best barbecue gurus.

## Don't get in a hurry.

The most common tip given to me was to take your time. Cooking good barbecue takes time and patience. Don't rush it. When I started cooking barbecue, I was told one to two hours per pound of meat. This can vary from smoker type to smoker type. It also can change from types of fuel used and the temperature of the smoker.

## Choose your wood wisely.

Type of wood used also came up many times. Around the South, hickory wood is most traditional. But other types of wood are used as well. Apple, oak, cherry, pear and more. If you're using a wood burning smoker, you will need to add wood about every 45 minutes or so.

## Start off easy.

Most pit masters agreed that for the beginner, burgers are a safe grilling bet. Then, when ready to smoke, start off with some chicken or a pork roast. Ribs, pulled pork, and tenderloins come down the road. Also, don't invite the family and friends over the first time you fire up the smoker.

## Marinate your meat.

Whenever possible, marinate your meat before cooking. I often marinate or season with a dry rub overnight.

## Learn the basics around the kitchen.

Learning to dice some veggies, make a sauce, and even boil some water will help out the beginner outdoor cook.

## Don't try too much at once.

Many legendary barbecue joints have really simple menus. "Keep it simple, stupid!" is what one pit master told me.

## Keep your smoke.

The secret to great smoky flavored barbecue is to keep your lid closed. Only open it when checking fuel, temperature or when basting. Just opening the lid to show off your brisket to buddies increases cooking time and loses your smoke!

## Keep the air flowing and the fire small.

Even though you have the lid closed, make sure you regulate the air flow to keep your fire going. Also keep your fire small when slow cooking. You are looking for smoke. As you change cooking methods from smoking to grilling, your heat source will get larger and move more directly underneath your food.

## Make small changes.

If you see something going wrong or you want to try something else, make only small changes. Making a huge firebox change or airflow change in the middle of a smoking session can ruin the best cut of meat. Make a small adjustment and go from there.

## Use seasoned wood.

When you start out, make sure to use seasoned wood for smoking. Green wood can be used by seasoned pros, but beginners should avoid it since it can cause a bitter taste. When using wood chips, be sure to soak them at least 30 minutes in water before using.

# Essential Barbecue Gadgets

**I asked several barbecue buddies this simple question.** "What 10 items does the backyard barbecue guru need?" Many of the answers included radios, a favorite CD, and cold adult beverages. While I do agree, I had to remind them that I was looking for cooking tips. "Ohhh, OK," seemed to be the usual response. By no means is this list complete, but it does offer a bit of insight to what you may want to pick up next time you're out shopping for grilling stuff. These are not in any particular order.

*A good basting brush is an essential barbecue tool.*

- Nothing beats a good **barbecue mop.**

- You can't get a mop without picking up a good **basting brush.**

- **Heat-resistant mitts** are a must-have for hot smokers and grills.

- Stop by a dollar store and pick up lots of **hand and dish towels.**

- Don't skimp here, buy a good pair of **cooking tongs.**

- A heavy-duty stainless steel **spatula**

- A great set of good **cutting knives** is a must.

- A cooking **timer**

- Lots of **heavy-duty foil**

- A good **remote thermometer**

# Some Not-So-Essential Gadgets

**Of course** when you ask a bunch of outdoor chefs about stuff they need to cook with, some really fun items are named. Here are a few that made the Not-So-Essential list.

- You've got to have a cooler filled with . . . "ahh . . . **beverages.**"

- Cindy in Virginia says, **"Brandy."**

- A **clean shirt** to change into.

- Several country, blues, or **Jimmy Buffet CDs.**

- Smoky John says, **"Significant other."**

- Bobby says, "Jelly donuts for a **midnight snack**."

- Several tailgate goers said, **"A football and frisbee."**

- Chad near Cherokee, North Carolina, says, "You have to have **garlic."**

- Randall in Johnson City, Tennessee, says, "A very **comfortable lawn chair."**

- Many people said that you had to have a **favorite, good luck, hat.**

# Caution! Handle with Care
## (Barbecue Safety)

**Food safety plays an important role in outdoor cooking.** In fact, when you think about it, more caution needs to be taken with outdoor cooking than any other method of cooking. So this brief section has a few tips on keeping your next shindig safe.

## Keep Meat Fresh

It all starts in the grocery store or butcher shop. When you're out shopping, buy cold food like meat and poultry last, right before checkout. Separate raw meat and poultry from other food in your shopping cart. Also use separate bags to hold meats so dripping doesn't cross-contaminate.

## Defrost Properly

Always thaw frozen meat in the fridge. Don't defrost meat on a counter top. Make sure the meat has completely defrosted before you begin to cook. This will ensure it cooks more evenly and that there are not pockets of undercooked areas inside the meat. You can also thaw meat in a microwave, but be sure to cook it as soon as possible. When thawing in cold water, place the meat in a zip-close bag.

## Safe Meat Marinating

Never ever re-use a marinade as a sauce unless it has been boiled first. Always discard leftover marinade after any cooking session or meal. Marinate your meat in a covered dish and always in the fridge.

## Transporting Food Safely

Always keep cold food cold and hot food hot. Place cold food right from the refrigerator into a cooler. Keep the cooler in the coolest part of the car. Always use a separate cooler for hot foods.

## Keep Things Clean

Always keep your cooking area, stoves, ovens, and grill clean.

## Wash Your Hands Often

Always wash your hands with soap and warm water before and after handling raw meat. You should also wash them before and after cooking.

## Use a Clean Towel

Many of us like to use a towel or just the front of our aprons to wipe our hands off. When cooking, consider using clean towels when you prep, when you cook, and when you are ready to serve. Paper towels work wonders as well.

## Cook Thoroughly

Always cook your meat to a safe internal temperature. Poultry should reach 180 degrees. Ground beef should reach 160 degrees. Ground chicken or turkey should cook to 170 degrees. Beef, veal, lamb steaks, roasts and chops can be cooked to 145 to 150 degrees. Pork should reach 160 degrees.

## Keep Hot Food Hot

Use a hot plate or covered warmer after cooking meat and poultry on the grill, and keep it hot (140 degrees or warmer) until served. This really applies if you are having a large event where people will eat in stages.

## Leftovers

Refrigerate leftovers promptly. Toss any food that has been left out for over two hours without being properly cooled or heated. I recommend using a container that fits the amount of food you have to store. Decreasing the amount of air in the container will keep your food fresher longer.

# Hot Off the Grill

When taking food off the grill, use a clean platter. To prevent food-borne illness, don't put cooked food on the same platter that held raw meat or poultry. Also, don't use the same utensils for raw and cooked meat.

# Reheating

Reheat cooked meat to an internal temperature of 160 degrees. This will kill any bacteria.

# Safe Smoking Temps

The temperature in a smoker should be maintained at 250 to 300 degrees for proper food safety. You should still use a food thermometer to be sure the food has reached a safe internal temperature.

# Safe Sauce

In general, any sauce should be refrigerated after use. Sauces that contain ingredients such as cream, sour cream, cream cheese or mayonnaise have a shorter shelf life than sauces with a vinegar base and should be chilled as quickly as possible after use. Your meat's marinade also makes a great sauce, but it is very important to boil it after the raw meat is removed and before using it as sauce.

# Always Preheat

You should always preheat your gas grill for five to 10 minutes before adding food. This will kill any possible bacteria that may be in the grill or on the grill grates.

# Burn Off Any Charcoal Fluid

If you use a charcoal lighting fluid, make sure all of it burns off before adding meat. Never add meat then add more fluid to your fire. The chemicals in lighter fluid will leave a bad taste in the meat, and it can't be all that good for you.

# Out of the Woods

**What would barbecue be without some wood?** In order to claim you are barbecuing, you simply must use wood. The flavor can not be produced any other way. I'm not knocking gas or charcoal, because I use all three. But a barbecue sandwich is only barbecue if you can get the taste and flavor produced by wood smoke. Remember my wife Jamie's barbecue rule. "If you can't see or smell the smoke, then it might not be good barbecue!"

You can find assorted woods on the internet from barbecue and grilling online stores. You can also check your local grill store, outdoor furniture/patio store, or the charcoal section of your local grocery, hardware or department store for prepackaged wood chunks and chips.

Of course there is a down side to using wood with the cooking process. Wood is heavy, harder to store, may take longer to reach

the temperature you need for cooking, often requires more space than a bag of charcoal, and may be harder to light than other heat sources.

The best time to try a new wood is not when you have 60 people coming over for a huge cookout. Try new woods in small batches before breaking them out for the masses. Every wood produces a different flavor. The flip side is that some woods can turn meat bitter quicker while some can even be overpowering.

When you decide to add wood to your cooking, always use fresh, seasoned woods. I love the flavor of hickory, but I also love to try other woods whenever I get a chance. If you are just starting out, then your best bet would be to smoke with hickory and/or mesquite. Nothing will ever come close to the smell of a hickory-stoked smoker or the taste of some hand-pulled barbecue from a smoked beef brisket. While the following list of woods may be helpful, you can never really tell until your try to cook with the wood itself.

### *Here is a list of wood types. It is by no means complete, but it is some good starter info.*

**ALDER** – Alder wood is a very nice wood with a sweet flavor. It is good with meats such as fish, pork and poultry.

**ALMOND** – Almond wood has a sweet smoke flavor. It, too, is great with chicken, fish, and pork.

**APPLE** – I love apple wood. It is mild with a slight fruity flavor. After lightning struck an apple tree in our yard, we had the perfect chance to try it. Now I'm hoping some more lightning will take a few more limbs off the tree.

**ASH** – Ash has good flavor, but it is a fast-burning wood. I like using ash wood with fish.

**BIRCH** – Birch wood is similar to maple and is often used with poultry.

**CEDAR** – Cedar wood is not the best for smoking, but if you ever get a chance to use it for a plank with seafood, give it a try. Just get a cedar plank and soak it in water for an hour or so. Lay your fish or chicken on the plank and place it in the smoker. The cedar will produce a nice flavor.

**CHERRY** – Be careful when using cherry wood. Some types of cherry trees such as the Choke cherry tree can produce a bitter flavor. But in general, cherry trees offer mild and fruity smoke flavors.

**CRAB APPLE** – Crab apple is very similar to apple wood.

**FIG** – Wood from a fig tree produces a light flavor.

**GRAPEVINES** – Grapevines produce a rich and fruity flavor. You can add grapevines to charcoal or other woods.

**JAKE SAYS —**
Whatever you do, don't try to cook with pine or any treated wood.

## WOOD TIPS

Do not use wood that is treated or may contain chemicals including wood from pallets and scrap lumber. Also avoid painted or decaying wood. I would never recommend using wood that has mold growing on it, but if you insist on giving it a try, pre-burn the wood outside of your smoker to remove mold and fungus. Whatever you do, don't cook with pine. It may ruin your meat with a deep bitter taste and it may also damage your equipment.

**HICKORY** – Hickory is the most common wood used for smoking. It is the wood that is most commonly associated with barbecue. The taste is deep and very distinctive.

**MAPLE** – Maple wood provides a distinct maple flavor. A friend of mine smoked some cheese and whole garlic cloves with it. Very nice.

**MESQUITE** – The other most popular wood for smoking is mesquite wood which produces a strong flavor associated with many Tex Mex dishes. It is good with beef, fish, chicken, and game.

**OAK** – All types of oak are great for grilling and smoking. The flavor is deep and rich. Just about any meat can be smoked with oak.

**CITRUS TREES** (orange, lemon and grapefruit) – Give citrus a try! Citrus trees produce a nice, mild smoky flavor.

**PEAR** – The same storm that damaged our apple tree, destroyed a pear tree in our yard. It had a nice, smoked flavor. I often used the chunks in my smaller smoker with charcoal.

**PECAN** – Pecan wood produces a sweet and mild flavor. Many people say it is very close in flavor to hickory.

**PEACH** – Great on most white or pink meats, including chicken, turkey, pork and fish. The flavor is milder and sweeter than hickory.

**PERSIMMON** – The persimmon tree produces a wood that has a mild flavor. If oversmoked, however, the flavor can become bitter.

**WALNUT** – Walnut wood produces a very thick and heavy flavor. If used alone, walnut can produce a bitter taste. Because of this, it is often used with lighter woods.

# How to Store Wood

Storing wood is simple. The key is allowing it to dry or season. After splitting wood, stack it allowing air pockets between the wood that will help it dry evenly. If you pack it too tightly the moisture will be trapped and mold will start to grow. Stack wood in a dry place, not a damp or shaded area. When you cut wood, lay a tarp down on the ground to collect the chips and chunks and even sawdust to use in your gas grill or smoke box.

# How to Store Packaged Wood

If you buy a bag of wood chunks, chips, or pellets make sure you use what you need and close the bag up securely to protect the remaining wood from moisture and bugs. Store-bought chips and such are already seasoned and ready to use.

# Commercial Chips and Chunks

When you buy commercial wood chips and chunks, make sure to follow the directions on the package. Most of the time you will have to presoak any chips or chunks, and place them in a wood chip smoke box. Many wood pellets do not have to be soaked, and water will actually ruin the product. If you are using a smoke box, make sure you purchase wood pieces small enough to fit inside. The lids have to fit back on properly to keep the airflow correct for proper smoke to be produced. If not, your chips will simply burst into flames producing little or no smoke.

# Smoking with Green Wood

Beginners should avoid green wood because it is has a huge water content. Experienced pit masters can use this to their advantage, but novice smokers may end up with a bitter taste.

# Combining Wood and Charcoal

Go for it! The way most people get into using wood is to simply add a few chunks of wood to a pile of charcoal. Eventually you will be using a smoke box filled with wood and no charcoal.

## Combining Wood and Gas

Many people think that gas and wood cannot be combined. It can. Add wood to your gas grill by using packaged wood chips and pellets with a cast iron smoke box. Place the chips in the smoke box and place the box over the heat source. Most smoke boxes have holes on top to allow just enough air in the box so the wood will smolder. You can also use heavy-duty aluminum foil or disposable aluminum pans, but I would get the cast iron box. Aluminum can break down and thinner foils will burn through which will cause the ash and burning chips to fall into your gas grill.

## Old Ash and Burning Charcoal

When using wood chips at a tailgate party, I carry a metal fireplace ash can. Dump the embers in the can and add some water. I usually take the ash home. But if you do dispose of the charcoal or ash at the tailgate sight, make sure it is completely out. Also, don't dump your coals into the parking lot or the grass before leaving. In many areas this is against the law.

## Adding Flavor to Your Smoke

Barbecue is all about flavor! Try adding spices, fruit, garlic, peppers and more, directly to your smoke box. I have a friend who adds squeezed lemons and limes to his water pan when he fires up the 'que! Heck, you can toss a few fresh cut oranges or grapes into the fire for added flavor. Get creative and try your own combinations of fruits and spices.

# Now We're Cookin'

# Shorty's Cafe

**37757 US Highway 11 • Valley Head, Alabama 35989**
**(256) 635-0245**

In the shadows of Lookout Mountain, sits a small restaurant called Shorty's Cafe. It is located in a refurbished old gas station that, according to Shorty's can-do-everything employee Peggy, "has been here for a very long time."

Shorty's Café is owned by Janet "Shorty" Burton and her husband. "He is taller than me and called me Shorty all the time, and it stuck," Janet said.

"We started as a café with all kinds of dishes. The barbecue is what we are known for now, and we just never took café off the name." The barbecue is pit smoked, pulled pork. Shorty's also offers chicken, catfish, and shrimp. But the customer favorite is the Killer Potato. "We sell a bunch of potatoes!" The potato is so popular that instead of describing what goes on it to every customer, there is a photo of one by the register.

Shorty's advice to the weekend barbecue chef? "Be sure to use fresh spices and foods, and make sure that you take pride in what you prepare." According to Shorty, or Janet, that is how come her customers keep coming back.

**GREAT EATS:** The Killer potato is great! You can get it with pork barbecue or chicken. The menu also has a full line of subs and a kids' menu.

**NEAT THING:** There are a lot of neat pictures on the walls at Shorty's. Make sure you check them out when you stop by.

# Sauces, Marinades and Rubs

**Believe it, it's true.** A perfect smoked pork butt or brisket can be ruined by covering it with a bad sauce! I know, I know . . . sad but true. Here is what can happen—you spend hours marinating meat, smoking it with select woods, perfecting temps, and when it's ready, it falls apart and melts in your mouth. But all your friends remember is the sauce. They might say, "Billy Ray does a good pork sandwich but can't say much for his sauce!" With this in mind, I recommend that you take a little care to find your perfect barbecue sauce, whether it be store bought, one from this book, or your own secret recipe.

A note of caution! As you will find out, many pit masters love to talk and give out advice. But when it comes to giving up their secret ingredients for private sauces, most tend to quietly "forget" a dash of something. In fact, I know several pit masters that added a few extra items to throw you off the trail. Don't ya love barbecue? Who knew cooking could be so sneaky?!

# BARBECUE SAUCES

**The great thing about barbecue sauce** is that no two sauces are the same. Sauces change as you move from the Appalachian Mountains of the East to the ocean waters of the West Coast. They also change from back porch to back porch. Some are almost totally vinegar and water combined with dashes of spices and pepper. Others have mustard, sugar, tomato sauce and more. Nothing is set in stone as far as your perfect sauce goes. Don't worry about making a mistake. Try a few variations. Add different spices until you get the flavor you are looking for.

## Basic Memphis-Style Sauce

*This recipe comes from Charles T. who lives just outside of Memphis, Tennessee. He told me that this is same recipe his grandfather used. Charles said, "The only thing that might be different is that Pappaw and his friends might have added a touch of white lightning to the sauce every once in a while."*

1 cup tomato sauce
1 cup vinegar
5 tablespoons Worcestershire
  sauce
2 tablespoons melted butter
½ small onion, chopped

Big dash black pepper
  (more if you want it hotter)
Big dash cayenne pepper
1½ teaspoons salt
½ cup water

Mix all ingredients together in large saucepan, bring to a quick boil, reduce heat and let simmer for 10 minutes.

## Easy Finishing Sauce

*The longer this sauce sits, the better it gets. My buddy in the Carolinas makes this sauce and then stores it in the back of the fridge for a week or so before using.*

1 cup apple cider vinegar
2 cups water
2 tablespoons salt

1 tablespoon brown sugar
1 teaspoon cayenne
1 teaspoon red pepper flakes

Mix all ingredients together. Store in the fridge until ready to use.

# Macee's Easy Sweet BBQ Sauce

*My son, Macee, is a master at making stuff from ketchup. Here is a version of his sauce.*

**1 cup ketchup**
**½ cup brown sugar**
**¼ cup orange juice**
**⅓ cup apple cider vinegar**

**2 tablespoons mustard**
**1 teaspoon Worcestershire sauce**
**1 teaspoon garlic powder**

You can add a bit of water if needed to thin it out.

## JAKE SAYS —

The easiest way to make your own barbecue sauce for the first time is to buy a bottle of sauce that you like and then add some "stuff."

## GRILLING TIP

A friend of mine does a great barbecue sauce that is simply a bottle of the store-bought kind with fine chopped onions and peppers and a bit of maple pancake syrup added. He also adds something else, but he won't confirm or deny that secret ingredient. I think it is a dash of spiced rum.

# Barbecue Capital of the World

## Lexington, North Carolina

**M**any people will tell you that if you are looking for real barbecue on the east side of the Mississippi and the Smoky Mountains, then you need to head to Lexington, North Carolina. Once there, you will notice a city sign that proudly proclaims the town as the Barbecue Capital of the World. That makes it official!

According to the Chamber of Commerce, North Carolina lawmakers officially designated Lexington as "The Hickory Smoked Barbecue Capital." And they take this pretty serious in town as you can tell by the number of barbecue restaurants located there. As one resident told me, "We have about one barbecue place for every family!"

*Besides heading to Lexington for great barbecue Restaurants stop by the area for their Barbecue Festival every year. North Carolina is filled with Festivals where you can expect to see smokers lined up like this producing great barbecue.*

According to the chamber, Lexington's barbecue history started like many other barbecue tales—as a way to feed people during church and political rallies. Before they knew it, barbecue cooking had become a daily thing, and the town was known as "The Barbecue Capital of the World."

A Barbecue Festival is held in Uptown Lexington each year. Over 400 exhibitors sell everything from handmade crafts to homemade fudge. And of course . . . barbecue.

For more information call the VERY helpful people at the Lexington Tourism Authority at 336-236-4218 or visit them on the web at www.visitlexingtonnc.com.

# Almost Lexington Barbecue Sauce

*Lexington, North Carolina, is considered by many to be the home of real barbecue. Just ask anybody from Lexington. Here is a version of Lexington-style barbecue sauce that is easy to make and only gets better while it sits in the fridge. Submitted by E. Taylor*

1 gallon water
1 quart ketchup
1 quart apple cider vinegar
4 tablespoons sugar
3 tablespoons salt

2 tablespoons black pepper
2 tablespoons crushed red pepper
1 tablespoon hot sauce

Combine everything in a big pot and bring to a boil. Use or save in jars in the fridge.

# Western Carolina BBQ Sauce

*A man named Gerald wrote his recipe down on a napkin for me when I visited a restaurant outside of Black Mountain, North Carolina. Gerald says store it only in glass bottles because he just does not like plastic bottles.*

1 cup apple cider vinegar
½ cup water
⅔ cup ketchup
3 tablespoons crushed pepper
4 tablespoons salt

4 tablespoons black pepper
2 tablespoons garlic
2 tablespoons onion powder
¼ cup chopped onion

This sauce is very similar to Eastern Carolina Sauce except for the addition of ketchup. Mix and simmer. Store in the fridge for a few days for added flavor.

# Carol's Carolina Vinegar Sauce

*A nice lady named Carol mailed this recipe to me after I was on "Emeril Live." She said, "any decent barbecue pork needs a more than decent vinegar sauce to finish it off."*

1 cup apple cider vinegar
⅔ cup water
3 tablespoons crushed
  red pepper
4 tablespoons salt

4 tablespoons black pepper
2 tablespoons garlic
2 tablespoons onion powder
¼ cup chopped onion

Mix, simmer, then cool. Pour the sauce in a jar and stick in the fridge for a week or longer. This is great for pouring over a big pulled pork sandwich.

# South Carolina Mustard Sauce

*Mustard is a classic ingredient to barbecue sauce. This simple mustard sauce is great on just about any barbecue.*

⅓ cup apple cider vinegar
1 cup water
⅔ cup yellow mustard
3 tablespoons salt

2 tablespoons black pepper
1 tablespoon steak sauce
¼ cup chopped onion

Mix all in a small saucepan and simmer. Great for basting pork, or mix thinner for a great marinade for ribs and such!

**A common ingredient** in many barbecue recipes is mustard. Many pit masters rub down meat with mustard, vinegar and other spices before smoking. Why mustard? Well, back when settlers came over to the New World, mustard was easily available. It was used as a spice, a food preservative and even for health reasons. The flavorful liquid we love on hot dogs is a modern version that is a combination of crushed mustard seeds, spices, water and vinegar.

# Parrot Head Barbecue Sauce

*I am a huge Jimmy Buffet fan. I came up with this sauce for a barbecue luau party we planned. It is simple to make and has tons of great flavor. I used it as a marinade and made some for a finishing sauce. I used it on chicken and on pork.*

1 orange
4 cloves garlic, minced
¼ cup chopped onion
1 (15-ounce) can crushed
   pineapple
1 lemon
2 shot glasses spiced rum

1 can tomato sauce
¼ cup soy sauce
¼ cup brown sugar
¼ cup apple vinegar
¼ cup maple syrup
1 teaspoon ground ginger

Zest the orange and place the zest in a large saucepan. Add garlic, onion and pineapple with juice; simmer for a few minutes. While that is simmering, slice the orange and lemon and add them to the pan. Add remaining ingredients and bring to a boil. Boil down for about 15 minutes, then simmer on low for about 15 minutes more. Chill and serve. You can leave the orange and lemon in or take them out before serving. I used this sauce on chicken and on pork.

# Sweet and Sour Orange BBQ Sauce

*Peel a few oranges and enjoy the citrus punch this sauce adds to your barbecue.*

1 small orange, peeled and
   crushed
¼ cup pepper sauce
¼ cup vinegar
¼ cup brown sugar

¼ cup ketchup
1 teaspoon ground ginger
1 teaspoon soy sauce
1 teaspoon minced garlic

Mix all and simmer in a pan. I have poured into a blender, blended, and used this mix with my injector as well.

# Double Cola Barbecue Sauce

*We love our soft drinks in the South. We make cakes, pies, brownies and now even barbecue sauces from a can of Double Cola. The recipe was given to me by a nice guy who worked for Double Cola. I met him while standing in line for a hot dog at a Chattanooga Lookouts baseball game. Of course we talked about grilling hot dogs, then barbecue and such.*

2 cans Double Cola
2 cups ketchup
½ cup mustard
¼ cup fine chopped onion

1 tablespoon minced garlic
1 tablespoon maple syrup
1 teaspoon flour

Mix all together, except flour, in a saucepan. Bring to a boil and stir in the flour to help thicken if needed. Chill before using.

# Tennessee Whiskey Sauce

*Just about anyone who knows me well, knows that I love a nice whiskey or bourbon—for cooking purposes only, of course. When Melissa told me she had a sauce made with whiskey, you can bet I was happy.*

½ cup apple cider vinegar
½ cup ketchup
⅓ cup water
¼ cup whiskey (or more)
¼ cup chopped onion

2 tablespoons salt
2 tablespoons pepper
2 tablespoons brown sugar
1 tablespoon soy sauce

Add a bit more brown sugar for flavor, if you want. This sauce should be slow simmered and cooked down. Remove from heat and cool to thicken.

# Double Cola

If you are from the South, chances are you have drunk a few ice cold Double Colas. According to my friends at the Double Cola Company in Chattanooga, Tennessee, the soda started in 1922. Charles D. Little and Joe Foster started the Good Grape Company, which later became the Double Cola Company. It is called Double Cola because in 1933, the 6-ounce bottles were increased to a HUGE 12-ounce bottle. Yep, double the cola!

Double Cola is considered a trend-setter in the soft drink business. They were the first to offer the larger bottle size. They were also the first cola company to start using applied color labels and were the first major soft drink to be marketed in a 16-ounce returnable bottle.

When Double-Cola began to introduce its new citrus flavored soda in 1956, they held an employee contest to name the beverage. According to Marisa Lynskey of Double-Cola, long-time employee Dot Myers had just returned with her husband from her favorite pastime . . . skiing. "Dot loves to ski so she entered the name Ski and it won!"

Double Cola and Ski are sold in over 17 countries and the list is growing. In fact, the cola is so popular outside of the United States that almost 85 percent of Double Cola sales are overseas.

For more info on Double Cola, the company history, fun facts and some recipes, visit Double Cola at www.double-cola.com.

# Owensboro Dark Sauce

*This recipe was given to me by E. Simmons, a fireman I met while hanging out in Owensboro, Kentucky, looking for barbecue. He said, "The darker the sauce, the better the sauce."*

¼ cup apple cider vinegar
½ cup ketchup
¼ cup Kentucky bourbon

¼ cup Worcestershire sauce
2 tablespoons pepper
2 tablespoons brown sugar

Combine all ingredients and simmer slowly until completely cooked down. Remove from heat and cool to thicken. As usual, you can add a little more brown sugar if you want a little more flavor.

# Butter Barbecue Sauce

*Butter makes this sauce great! It is delicious for basting, topping, finishing and dipping. Submitted by C. Harding – Virginia*

1 cup melted butter
¼ cup water
2 teaspoons Worcestershire
  sauce
1 tablespoon lemon juice

1 teaspoon hot sauce
2 teaspoons sugar
1 teaspoon salt
1 teaspoon flour

Mix all ingredients and bring to a boil in a saucepan; let it cool. If needed, add a bit more flour to thicken. This sauce is for dipping chicken, fried taters and such.

# Quick Butter & Honey Barbecue Sauce

1 cup store-bought barbecue
  sauce
½ cup melted butter
⅓ cup honey

1 tablespoon vinegar
1 tablespoon any citrus juice
Dash ginger
Dash garlic

Mix all in a saucepan and simmer. Let cool to thicken.

# EASY WING SAUCES

**Barbecue chicken is a great thing.** My grills and smokers are often covered with chicken thighs, wings and legs. A nice lady told me one day that she remembered when wings were the parts of the chicken they tossed out. "They used to be the cheapest part of the bird." Somebody in Buffalo figured out that if you fried some wings and covered them in sauce, you could sell them like crazy. Here are a few sauces perfect for your next batch of wings.

# KILLER Hot Sauce!

*Making a great hot sauce is easy: mix some cayenne pepper, vinegar, water, and other spices together, and let it sit in the back of the fridge for a while. Making KILLER Hot Sauce requires a bit more energy and a few more ingredients, but it is still easy. I got the idea for this recipe from a gent who emailed me a question on my website. Combining his ingredients and a few more of my own, I came up with this KILLER sauce. You can adjust the heat level by adding more pepper, of course.*

1 small white onion, minced
1 small red onion. minced
1 tablespoon minced garlic
1 tablespoon veggie oil
2 cups water
1/3 cup minced carrots
4 habanero peppers, minced

4 tablespoons lime juice
2 tablespoons lemon juice
2 tablespoons apple cider
   vinegar
1 can tomato paste
1 teaspoon salt
1 teaspoon pepper

Add onions, garlic, and veggie oil to a saucepan and sauté. Combine with water and carrots and boil for about 5 minutes, or long enough to soften carrots. Add remaining ingredients (do not drain water from carrots) and pour into a blender. Blend until all ingredients are smooth.

# Easy Hot Wing Sauce

1 (3-ounce) bottle hot sauce
½ cup melted butter
2 tablespoons water
4 tablespoons maple syrup
¼ cup brown sugar
1 teaspoon salt

Mix all ingredients in a saucepan and bring to a boil, then let cool. Toss with wings.

# Ketchup Wing Sauce

1 cup ketchup
¼ cup vinegar
¼ cup hot sauce
¼ cup brown sugar

Mix all ingredients in a saucepan and bring to a boil, then let cool. Toss with wings.

# Ginger Almond Wing Sauce

1 cup white wine
½ cup chopped almonds
½ cup melted butter
¼ cup chopped red bell pepper
2 tablespoons lemon juice
1 teaspoon ground ginger
Dash salt and pepper

Mix all and toss with wings.

# Orange Marmalade Wing Sauce

*A great wing sauce with a bit of zesty citrus flavor.*

2 cups orange marmalade
½ cup Dijon mustard
½ cup water
1 teaspoon crushed red pepper
Dash salt
Dash thyme

Mix all ingredients in a saucepan and cook over very low heat until marmalade melts. Toss with wings.

# Mountain Man Wing Sauce

*This sauce will bring out the Appalachian Mountain Man in you—even if you never knew you had it. The sauce is strong and it is hot. A nice man I met visiting the mountains around Asheville, North Carolina, gave me this sauce, saying, "It takes a real man to eat this stuff, buddy." Ya got to love wing sauce recipes from people that dare you to make them.*

2 (3-ounce) bottles hot sauce
½ cup pancake syrup
  ("Not that sissy diet stuff!")
¼ cup brewed coffee
  ("The older the better")
¼ cup minced onion

¼ cup soy sauce
2 tablespoons chili powder
1 tablespoon crushed red
  pepper
1 teaspoon cumin powder

Mix all. Coat your wings. And eat up . . . if you dare.

## Deck Chef Tip!

### Toss Them Wings

However you cook your wings, try tossing them in the sauce of your choice. Cook your chicken. Then place them in a bowl you can cover and pour your sauce over the chicken. Attach the cover as tight as possible and shake and rotate the container until all of the chicken is covered in sauce. Be careful not to overfill the container because you want to allow enough tumble space for the sauce and chicken to mix well. If it seems easier, just brush on your sauce as your chicken wings cook.

# Pierce's Pitt Bar-B-Que

**447 Rochambeau Drive • Williamsburg, Virginia 23188**
**(757) 565-2955 • www.pierces.com**

In 1971, Julius C. Pierce, Sr., at age 57, decided to start his own business. Not afraid of hard work, he had helped raise his brothers and sisters, worked on the railroads as a cook, and traveled the country.

"He opened the restaurant with 40 borrowed dollars in a small box instead of a cash register," said Pierce's director of operations, Andrea Hutchenson.

Today, Pierce's is well known as a good place to eat. "We use hickory and oak in our pits," Hutchenson said. The smoking process can take anywhere from eight to 13 hours. "Rain or shine, our pit guys are out there. They get cold and wet in the winter and get hot as heck in the summer!" Hutchenson said.

They use only pork shoulders known as Boston Butts. These are slow cooked over wood burning outdoor pits. When done, the meat is pulled from the bone by hand and mixed with their own tomato-vinegar based secret sauce.

**GREAT EATS:** Pierce's offers a HUGE menu—pork, ribs, double grilled chicken, catfish, dinner rolls, plate dinners, sandwiches, a full kids' menu, and more. Be sure to try a sweet potato stick! And save room for dessert—homemade cookies, fudge walnut brownies, cakes, and cobbler.

**NEAT THING:** The word pit on the sign outside of Pierce's Pitt Bar-B-Que is spelled wrong. (Pit only has one "t.") "The sign was painted by an elderly man," Hutchenson said. "When he finished, Julius said out loud that pit was spelled wrong. The elderly painter picked up his stuff, turned to Julius, and politely said, 'If ya don't like it, then fix it yourself.' He decided to keep it the way it was."

# CHICKEN WHITE SAUCES

**White sauces can be used with other meats,** but they are best suited for chicken—baked, fried, smoked or however you prepare it. They also make great dipping sauces. Here are a few quick sauces perfect for a big plate of chicken. Most often I find specialized versions of white sauce down around Alabama.

## White BBQ Sauce

*The first time I ever had white BBQ sauce, I was amazed at the flavor it added to smoked chicken. These special sauces can be found all over now, but it is often associated with Alabama, Mississippi, Florida and the rest of the Delta area. I have been told that it has close ties to tartar sauce.*

1½ cups mayonnaise
⅓ cup apple cider vinegar
¼ cup lime juice
2 tablespoons sugar

2 tablespoons cracked black pepper
2 tablespoons white Worcestershire sauce

Mix all ingredients and chill before serving.

## White Hot BBQ Sauce

*My brother Scot turned me onto white hot barbecue sauce. He and a bunch of guys worked a great barbecue restaurant just across the street from Vanderbilt football stadium in Nashville, Tennessee. Scot has yet to let go of the secret to White Hot Barbecue Sauce, so I had to come up with one of my own.*

1 cup mayonnaise
2–4 tablespoons cider vinegar
2 tablespoons freshly grated or prepared horseradish
2 tablespoons water

1 teaspoon coarse salt
½ teaspoon freshly ground black pepper
¼ teaspoon cayenne pepper

Combine all of the ingredients in a bowl, and whisk until smooth. If you make this sauce a day or two before you need it, store in the fridge and the flavor will be wonderful.

# Old Fashioned Alabama White Barbecue

1 clove garlic, minced
1 cup mayo
1½ tablespoon red wine
  vinegar

1 teaspoon fresh thyme
¼ teaspoon cayenne pepper
1 teaspoon yellow mustard
Salt and pepper to taste

Combine until smooth and store in fridge until needed.

## JAKE SAYS —

White sauces made from mayo or sour cream are best used only once, then disposed of.

# Honey White Sauce

1 cup mayo
2 tablespoons lemon juice
3 tablespoons honey
3 tablespoons white wine
vinegar
1 teaspoon salt
1 teaspoon pepper

Mix all ingredients in a small glass bowl and stir until smooth. Chill and serve.

# SAUCES FOR FISH AND SEAFOOD

**Even though** this book is based on barbecue in the Smoky Mountain area, there is still plenty of room for some seafood sauces. I have tried some great trout, largemouth bass, catfish and many pan fish from ponds, rivers and streams around the mountains, all with great marinades and sauces. But, like many families around the South, we head to the Coast several times a year for some great seafood. Don't be surprised if the sauce you make for a big chunk of corn meal-battered fried catfish is also great for some sea bass or grouper.

## Coastal Carolina Fish Sauce

*I have eaten so much fish over the years that I tend to find myself stuck in a tartar sauce rut. A nice lady in a hotel restaurant had fun with me trying to guess what the heck was in her sauce. When I got close, she let me in on a few key ingredients. Here is a sauce that will make your seafood swim with flavor.*

2 tablespoons olive oil
2 tablespoons lemon juice
¼ cup fine chopped
   sun-dried tomatoes
1 tablespoon sugar

1 tablespoon parsley
Dash allspice
Dash salt
Dash pepper

Mix all together in a bowl. Cover and chill. Before cooking fish, brush with sauce and cover for an hour or so in the fridge. Perfect for grilling, smoking or baking.

# Alabama Grill

**2050 Parkway • Pigeon Forge, Tennessee 37863**
**(865) 908-877**

**539 Opry Mills Drive • Nashville, Tennessee 37214**
**(615) 514-7000**

**8341 Concord Mills Blvd. • Concord, North Carolina 28027**
**(704) 979-700**

JEFF COOK
ALABAMA
VOCALS, GUITAR & FIDDLE

When I started this book, my friend Robin said she had a buddy that loved a great steak, and that I should give him a call. Jeff Cook, guitar player, vocals and more for the legendary band Alabama, has done a bunch of traveling. The band has played in about every state and in many countries. According to Jeff, time is often the main factor when picking a place to eat while on the road.

"If the schedule permits, and I can get out to get something to eat . . . nothing beats a big ol' steak."

At one time Jeff owned a small restaurant in Alabama that specialized in Southern-style meat-and-threes. "It was a great restaurant and I got it so we'd have a place to play close to home," he said. The band now lends their name to a chain of theme restaurants called Alabama Grill.

As you might guess, the place is made for Alabama fans as well as people who like to eat. The menu contains a wide variety of foods. Everything from traditional, country-style, and meat-and-three-style dinners to fresh-cut steaks grilled how you like them. Of course, they also offer some great ribs, hickory-smoked hand-pulled pork platters and more. The food, combined with the Alabama theme makes for a neat place to eat.

**GREAT EATS:** Try the Barbecue Shrimp with Bama Bourbon Glaze, or Jeff Cook's signature chicken dish.

**NEAT THING:** Expect a very healthy dose of country music, and cool memorabilia all over the walls. There's a stage inside, and the band has been known to stop by and play a few songs when in town.

# Jeff Cook's Emerald Coast Cocktail Sauce

*Today, in addition to playing with his band Alabama, Jeff concentrates on his music studio where the best musicians and hopeful future superstars come to record their albums. For more information about Jeff and his studio, visit his web site at www.jeffcookenterprises.com. While you're there, visit his online store and check out his Emerald Coast Sauce. Jeff says it is "perfect for seafood, beef, chicken, pork and even wild game."*

**4 tablespoons Jeff Cook's Emerald Coast Sauce**

**1 tablespoon catsup**
**1 tablespoon horseradish**

Mix all the ingredients together. You can add a dash of garlic, salt and pepper, if you want

# Butter and Olive Oil Dipping Sauce

*This sauce is great for dipping seafood and fresh French bread.*

**½ cup melted butter**
**¼ cup extra virgin light olive oil**

**1 tablespoon garlic powder**
**1 tablespoon oregano**

Mix and serve.

# Florida Seafood BBQ Sauce

**½ cup butter, melted**
**½ cup lemon juice**
**½ cup white wine**

**1 tablespoon Cajun all spice**
**1 tablespoon fine chopped scallions**

Combine all ingredients well. Great on broiled and grilled seafood.

# Hot Catfish Sauce

*There is a whole bunch of catfish eaten around these parts. Here is a nice hot tartar sauce perfect for some catfish.*

**1 cup mayonnaise**
**¼ cup hot pepper sauce**
**2 tablespoons relish**
**1 teaspoon lemon juice**

**1 teaspoon prepared**
  **horseradish**
**Salt and pepper to taste**

Mix all ingredients in a bowl and chill before serving.

# Mountain Lake Bass Barbecue Sauce

*A friend of mine once told me, "What good is fishin' if ya can't cook 'em good?" Here is a great recipe for a sauce that makes bass, or any fish, worth the catch. Submitted by John C.*

**6 tablespoons unsalted butter,**
  **melted**
**2 teaspoons fresh minced garlic**
**2 tablespoons ketchup**

**1 tablespoon thyme**
**Dash of sugar, pepper and**
  **paprika**

This sauce is a great baste when grilling fish fillets. You'll also love it at your next fish fry.

*My buddy Stan and the rest of his family enjoy their traditional holiday meal at Hickory Log Barbecue in North Carolina.*

# MARINADES AND STEAK SAUCES

**Nothing beats a marinade!** I don't care if you are a weekend griller, longtime smoker or master chef. We all know the importance of marinades. The way marinades work is simple. Most contain an acid such as vinegar and oil plus lots of spices. The acid breaks down the tissue, while the oil carries the flavor of the spices.

## Kent's Tasty Jerk Marinade

*This is a great, basic marinade recipe that can also be used for basting or injecting. My son loves it for dipping some nacho chips into.*

1 (8-ounce) can pineapple
  chunks in juice
½ cups firm packed brown
  sugar
4 tablespoons soy sauce
4 tablespoons red wine vinegar
1 tablespoon cumin powder
1½ tablespoons Cajun
  seasoning

1½ tablespoons garlic powder
2 teaspoons cayenne pepper
1 teaspoon black pepper
1 teaspoon salt
1 teaspoon onion powder
½ teaspoon thyme
2 tablespoons hot sauce
2 tablespoons lime juice
2 tablespoons lemon juice

Mix all in a blender and blend well. If using with an injector, make sure to blend extra fine so your needle does not clog up.

## Beer Marinade

*Of course I have to have a recipe for beer in this section. When you go to a barbecue cook-off, it is amazing how many people use beer in the cooking process . . . besides taking a few sips!*

1 can beer
½ cup vinegar
¼ cup brown sugar
2 tablespoons cayenne pepper

1 tablespoon crushed red
  pepper
1 tablespoon lemon juice

Mix well and enjoy.

# Italian Dressing Marinade

*If you want to make a really easy and great marinade, try this recipe. If you want an even easier and quicker version, just use a bottle of Italian dressing.*

1 cup Italian dressing
½ cup soy sauce
½ cup wine vinegar
¼ cup Worcestershire sauce
2 tablespoons mustard

2 teaspoons salt
1 tablespoon coarsely ground
  pepper
2 teaspoons chopped parsley
2 cloves garlic, crushed

Mix all and cover. Chill before using.

## JAKE SAYS —

If you're short on time and need a good marinade, open a bottle of salad dressing. Creamy dressings, like ranch, are perfect marinades for chicken and fish. Those with oil and vinegar are better for pork and beef.

# Apple Cider Marinade

2 cups apple cider
1 teaspoon honey
2 tablespoons hot sauce
Large dash salt
2 teaspoons Dijon-style mustard
Large dash pepper

Mix well, and it's ready to go on your favorite fish.

# Fish Marinade

*This is a very delicate wine marinade for just about any fish. It has just a touch of garlic. This is a nice play off the flavor of the wine. I like to use a fruity wine, but pick a wine that you already enjoy.*

**1 cup white wine**
**2 tablespoons soy sauce**

**1 teaspoon lemon juice**
**1 large dash garlic powder**

Mix, brush on fish, marinate for about 30 minutes of so—an hour tops.

# Asian Marinade

*Many of my friends know that when I am not eating barbecue or chicken, I can often be found at a decent Chinese restaurant or a Japanese steak house. This recipe is an Americanized version of a steak marinade.*

**¼ cup cooking sherry**
**¼ cup pineapple juice**
**2 tablespoons soy sauce**
**2 tablespoons brown sugar**

**2 tablespoons hoisin sauce**
**1 tablespoon black pepper**
**1 teaspoon ginger**

Mix well and use to marinate your favorite seafood.

# Peanut Marinade

**3 tablespoons peanut oil**
**1 tablespoon peanut butter**
**2 cloves garlic, minced**
**1 tablespoon minced onion**
**⅔ cup ketchup**
**½ cup cider vinegar**
**¼ cup Worcestershire sauce**

**2 tablespoons lemon juice**
**1 teaspoon lime juice**
**1 teaspoon ginger**
**1 teaspoon mustard**
**¼ cup honey**
**2 tablespoons brown sugar**

Mix all and marinate your meat. You can also whip some up and use it as a baste.

# Big Tom Price

## Big Show Foods, and John Boy and Billy's Grillin' Sauce

The smell of barbecue and grilled chicken combined with the sound of music and laughter . . . you may very well be near a Big Show Foods Fan Zone event.

The Fan Zone is a place where fans of all sports can come, have a good time, meet the John Boy and Billy Big Show Grilling Team and enjoy free food and cold beverages. According to Tom Price of Big Show Foods, "We set up in towns throughout the radio network to say thanks to all of the customers of Big Show Foods and to say thanks to all of the great fans of the John Boy and Billy Big Show."

Fred Overman, cook-for-the-day Macee Whitaker, and Big Tom Price of Big Show Foods, take a break from cooking for a Fan Zone event in Nashville, Tennessee. Thanks to their efforts, hundreds of hungry race fans consumed barbecue, grilled chicken, and burgers seasoned with John Boy and Billy's Grillin' Sauce and John Boy and Billy's Marinade.

Big Tom, as he is called by radio fans, says, "The Fan Zone has traveled all around the Appalachian area including the Carolinas, Tennessee, Kentucky, Virginia and many other Big Show states. We know our barbecue! It HAS to be good. If John Boy and Billy fans are happy with the food we serve, then I know they will enjoy our sauces and marinades found at www.bigshowfoods.com and local retailers." For one afternoon, my son Macee and I volunteered as Big Show Foods Grill Team Members, so I can guarantee the food is great.

The next time you are at a local race track or grocery store, don't be surprised if you hear Big Show Foods Grill Team member Fred Overman let loose a with loud howdy. "Hey! Ya'll want some free barbecue and chicken?" If you do see The Fan Zone, definitely head over for some good fun and great 'que.

# Big Show Emergency Marinade

*My buddy Big Tom Price of the* **John Boy and Billy Big Show** *and www.bigshow-foods.com says, with a big smile, you should* "always use John Boy and Billy Grillin' Sauce. But if you're in a pinch here is something I do to marinate chicken!"

**2 cups apple cider vinegar**
**1 tablespoon salt**
**1 tablespoon sugar**
**1 tablespoon cayenne pepper**

**1 tablespoon black pepper**
**½ tablespoon crushed**
 **red pepper**
**Ketchup, if desired**

Combine all ingredients in a glass bowl and "Stick your chicken in it overnight." Keep in the fridge until ready to cook.

## Deck Chef Tip!

### Marinating Meat

Marinades tenderize and flavor meat. But they do not completely tenderize tough meat. For additional tenderizing, use a tenderizing tool or add yogurt or pineapple juice to your marinade. Yogurt contains enzymes that help break down the meat fibers. Marinades need three hours or more to work properly for tough meats. Chicken requires only about an hour or so before the marinade works. And seafood should only stay in a marinade for about 30 minutes.

# Yogurt Marinade

*Yogurt? Yep. Any marinade made with yogurt is great on more fragile meats such as poultry and fish. The yogurt has enzymes that help tenderize the meat without overpowering it. Flavored yogurt also adds great taste.*

1 cup plain yogurt
¼ cup extra virgin olive oil
2 tablespoons hot sauce
4 cloves minced garlic

1 teaspoon lemon juice
1 teaspoon dried mint leaves
Salt and pepper

Combine all in a blender and mix well. Perfect for seafood and poultry. Make sure you marinate your meat in the fridge when using yogurt.

# Pineapple Marinade

*Anytime you use pineapple in a recipe, you can just about count on me eating a bunch. I love the flavor of pineapple. In this marinade, it makes just about any meat fantastic.*

1 large can pineapple chunks
   with juice
¼ cup jalapeño peppers
2 tablespoons minced garlic
1 cup pineapple or orange juice
½ cup fresh lime juice
¼ cup chopped fresh cilantro

¼ cup chopped onion
1 tablespoon cumin powder
2 tablespoons black pepper
2 teaspoons lime zest
2 teaspoons salt
1 tablespoon honey

Mix and toss it in a blender for a few seconds.

# Homemade Steak Sauce

*Everybody loves a great steak sauce to top a nice, juicy steak. But what makes a great steak sauce? Just about anything you want. Here is a recipe that makes a very nice, deep flavored steak sauce. Like many other sauces with long histories, steak sauce was developed to hide the taste of some meat. Yep, back in the good old days, blends of vinegar, juices, spices and more became steak sauce.*

1 cup ketchup
3 tablespoons brown sugar
⅔ cup minced onion
5 cloves fresh garlic, minced
¼ cup water
¼ cup Worcestershire sauce

¼ cup lemon juice
¼ white wine
2 tablespoons soy sauce
1 tablespoon mustard
¼ teaspoon ground clove
¼ teaspoon cinnamon

Place all in a blender and blend well. Store in the fridge.

## JAKE SAYS —

Here is a very simple steak sauce that can be made from easy-to-get ingredients.

# Jake's Simple Steak Sauce

⅓ cup Worcestershire sauce
1½ teaspoons minced garlic
⅓ cup ketchup
1 teaspoon salt
1 tablespoon vinegar
Large dash pepper
1 tablespoon onion powder

Mix and eat. It doesn't get any easier.

# Grilling Steak Sauce

1 small can chopped
  mushrooms, mashed
2 tablespoons melted butter
1 beef bullion cube
¼ small onion, diced

½ cup red wine
2 tablespoons flour
1 teaspoon salt
1 teaspoon pepper
½ teaspoon hot sauce

Boil, let cool, and brush on steaks while grilling. I like to mash the mushrooms with a fork.

# Mountain Ramp and Wine Sauce

*Here is a great recipe I made using ramps, which are actually leeks and are very similar to an onion. Ramps are a great plant found around the Appalachian foothills.*

1 cup white wine
½ cup fine chopped ramps
¼ cup extra-virgin olive oil
2 tablespoons butter

2 tablespoons light corn syrup
1 teaspoon lemon juice
Salt and pepper to taste

Combine all ingredients and simmer in a saucepan to cook off the alcohol.

**Ramps** can be found along the foothills of the Southern Appalachians. It is kind of a cross between an onion and a leek. The harvest time for ramps is generally in early spring. What makes a ramp great? The flavor! The flavor is deep and distinctive. If you get a chance, stop by one of the regional ramp festivals from Tennessee to the Carolinas for ramp eating contests, recipe contests, baking contests and, of course, some great outdoor cooking!

# RUBS AND SUCH

**Rubs are simply combinations of spices** rubbed onto and pressed into meats before cooking. Rubs are dry marinades, in a sense. BUT WAIT, barbecue nuts. RUBS CAN BE WET! Yep, a wet rub is a rub that has a few drops of liquid, often a citrus juice or vinegar, added to make a paste. Call it a dry marinade or a wet rub. Who cares? They work great!

## Kent's Basic Rub

*This is my basic rub recipe. I also put it in a shaker bottle and use it as a seasoning.*

4 tablespoons freshly ground
  black pepper
4 tablespoons paprika
2 tablespoons garlic powder

2 teaspoons salt
2 teaspoons brown sugar
2 teaspoons chili powder

Combine all ingredients; rub thoroughly into meat before cooking.

## Quick Jerk Wet Rub

6 green onions, minced
2 teaspoons minced Scotch
  Bonnet pepper
4 cloves garlic, minced
¼ cup vegetable oil
¼ cup fresh lime juice

1 tablespoon apple cider vinegar
2 tablespoons soy sauce
1 teaspoons thyme
1 teaspoon chili powder
Dash of salt and pepper

Mix all ingredients together and press the wet rub into the meat you are going to cook. Allow the meat to rest before cooking.

**Note:** The Scotch Bonnet Pepper is a staple of any good Jerk rub or marinade. Most larger grocery stores carry them. If you don't have any laying around, use your favorite hot pepper or even some crushed red pepper.

# Tex Mex Rub

*This rub recipe has a bit of a kick to it. I love it!*

3 tablespoons paprika
¼ cup brown sugar
¼ cup sugar
1½ tablespoons cayenne
  pepper

1 tablespoon cumin powder
1½ teaspoons chili powder
1½ teaspoons ground pepper
Dash of crushed red pepper

Combine all ingredients; rub thoroughly into meat before cooking.

# Horseradish Rub

*Simple and easy. Try this rub on a few chicken breasts when you are looking for some ZING!*

¼ cup horseradish
1 tablespoon chili powder
1 tablespoon lemon zest

1 teaspoon garlic
½ teaspoon salt

Combine all ingredients; rub thoroughly into meat before cooking.

# Caribbean Jerk Rub

*Jerk rubs offer great taste with heat. A great combination of flavor and taste.*

3 tablespoons allspice
2 tablespoons minced scallion
1 tablespoon nutmeg
1 teaspoon clove
1 teaspoon pepper
1 tablespoon cumin powder

1 teaspoon chili powder
1 teaspoon ground pepper
Dash thyme
Dash crushed red pepper
Zest lime or lemon

Combine all ingredients; rub thoroughly into meat before cooking.

# Kentucky Mint Rub

*I was born in Kentucky and have spent a large amount of time working in Lexington, Kentucky. This rub has the taste of mint. A bit different, but a nice twist to your basic rubs.*

¼ cup brown sugar
¼ cup sugar
1 tablespoon mint

Dash thyme
2 tablespoons garlic powder
Salt and pepper to taste

Combine all ingredients; rub thoroughly into meat before cooking.

# Pork Salt Rub

*An easy rub for pork that combines traditional seasonings with a bit of flare. While the spices tend to add a bit of heat and tons of flavor, the brown sugar adds a nice sweet taste. Be careful not to burn meat that has sugar in the rub or the sauce, because it may add a bitter taste to your meat.*

4 tablespoons salt
3 tablespoons brown sugar
2 tablespoons paprika
1 tablespoon cayenne pepper

1 tablespoon cumin powder
1 teaspoon chili powder
1 teaspoon ground pepper
1 teaspoon dry mustard

Combine all ingredients; rub thoroughly into meat before cooking.

# Spicy Seafood Rub

*A rub for seafood? Yep, even delicate meats can be rubbed. This rub can be used on just about any fish. But don't hesitate to try other ingredients.*

¼ cup black pepper
2 tablespoons Cajun seasoning
2 tablespoons allspice
1 tablespoon paprika

4 teaspoons cayenne pepper
4 teaspoons chili powder
2 teaspoons garlic powder

Combine all ingredients; rub thoroughly into meat before cooking.

# Buttery Steak Spread

*Sometimes all you need is some butter for a great steak sauce. Try this recipe out next time you toss a few steaks on the grill.*

**3 tablespoons butter or
  margarine
1 teaspoon steak sauce**

**½ teaspoon minced garlic
½ teaspoon black pepper
½ teaspoon sugar**

Mix it all up, and spread on your steak when you turn it.

# Sweet Wet Rub

*A wet rub is a rub that is a basic dry rub with a bit of moisture added to form a paste or relish consistency.*

**2 tablespoons yellow mustard
½ cup brown sugar
1 tablespoon paprika**

**1 tablespoon minced onion
1 teaspoon soy sauce
⅓ cup beer**

Combine dry ingredients in a bowl; add soy sauce. Mix well. Slowly pour in the beer and stir until you have a thick paste. Spoon and rub on meat. Wrap in cling wrap and store in the fridge.

# Beef

**Bring on the BEEF!** Pork is king in the South. Chicken is popular across the country. But when you pass over the Mighty Mississippi River something happens to barbecue. Beef is king out west! The flavor of the Southwest is mingled with the flavor and traditions of the East. So with that in mind, it's time for some beef recipes.

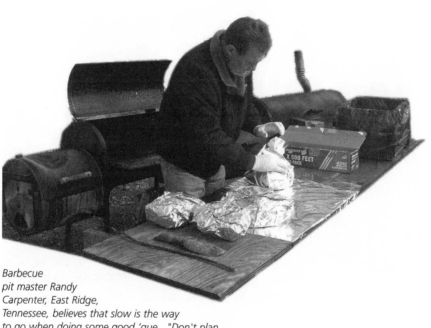

*Barbecue pit master Randy Carpenter, East Ridge, Tennessee, believes that slow is the way to go when doing some good 'que. "Don't plan on rushing it!" Randy says. He also suggests using the freshest wood possible. "It makes a difference in taste. It makes it more consistent."*

# The Easiest Steaks in the World

Ever wonder what a plain ol' steak tastes like? If you're looking for a simple steak with little fuss and lots of flavor then try this. First, get your local meat department to cut you the freshest steaks possible. Any cut will do, but try for something with some fat for juice. Take them home and rub with a bit of salt and pepper, place in the fridge while you get the grill going. Grill them as soon as possible. As you turn, sprinkle with a bit more salt and pepper and brush with a very small amount of butter. Turn only once. Let rest a few minutes and serve hot!

## Deck Chef Tip!

### Grilling Steaks

My wife has to remind me of this because I like to "fiddle" with stuff. Leave the steaks alone when you are grilling them. Turn your grilled steaks only once. Here is the chart for 1-inch steaks over high heat:

2 to 3 minutes per side for rare
3 to 5 minutes per side for medium
5 to 8 minutes per side for well done

Just before you remove your steaks from the grill add a dash of salt and pepper and brush with a very light coat of your favorite marinade. Before serving, allow the steaks to rest for about 5 minutes after removing from heat.

# Grilled Dijon Glazed Porterhouse

3 or 4 porterhouse steaks
¼ cup Dijon mustard
1 tablespoon lemon juice
1 tablespoon minced garlic

1 teaspoon ginger
½ teaspoon salt
½ teaspoon pepper
Dash of thyme

Combine all of your ingredients (except steak) in a bowl and mix well. Brush both sides of the steaks with the mix and place the steaks in a glass dish; cover as tight as possible. Place in the fridge for as long as possible (preferably overnight) before cooking. I cook these steaks over medium-high heat on the grill using charcoal and hickory chunks. Brush remaining marinade over steaks as they cook.

# Rosemary Butter New York Strips

4 new york strips
2 tablespoons olive oil
2 tablespoons rosemary

2 tablespoons butter
Salt and pepper to taste

Brush steaks with olive oil and allow the steak to rest for as long as possible. Rub in rosemary and place on grill. Melt butter and baste lightly as you turn. Cook to desired doneness. Salt and pepper to taste. Serve hot.

# Horseradish Steaks

2 large, tender steaks
½ cup Worcestershire sauce
2 tablespoons yogurt

1 tablespoon prepared
  horseradish
1 teaspoon black pepper

Combine all of the ingredients except for the steak in a glass bowl for your marinade. Add in the steaks, cover and marinate as long as possible. (Yogurt-based marinades work best over a long period of time.) Grill the steaks to perfection turning once or as few times as possible. Remove from heat when done and allow to rest for several minutes before serving.

# Pit Stop Pam

## Mountains, NASCAR, Friends and "A Grill!"

Pam and her husband Roger consider themselves die-hard NASCAR fans. When Pam talks about NASCAR you can see the light in her eyes. According to Pam, Bristol offers the best seats in NASCAR. But Pam and Roger don't stop in the Appalachian foothills of Tennessee and Virginia. They have been to races in North Carolina at Lowe's Motor Speedway, Talladega

Super Speedway in Alabama and of course the big daddy of NASCAR Daytona International Motor Speedway.

When they go to the races, Pam and Roger always camp out which means they grill a lot. "We cook breakfast, lunch, dinner and snacks on the grill," Pam said. Breakfast ranges from easy stuff to full blown menus including bacon, eggs, sides, homemade biscuits and more. Of course when dinnertime comes around, the campground becomes a huge tailgate kitchen full of barbecue, hot dogs, burgers, seafood and shrimp. And no race weekend would be complete without Pam's Bristol Steaks (see recipe on opposite page).

According to Pam, the way to make sure every meal is great, fun, and easy is to follow the old saying, "Keep it simple." Barbecue and grilling recipes for tailgate parties or tailgate living should use as few ingredients as possible while getting all of the flavor.

"For us, going to a race is a big deal. The whole campground becomes one big neighborhood—one big family. We've met people from across the country while at the races." By the way, in addition to her cooking tip, Pam offered this advice: "Pull for Dale Earnhardt, Jr.!"

# Pam's Bristol Steaks

**2 steaks**
**1 zip close bag**

**1 bottle white wine**
**Salt and Pepper to taste**

Place your steaks in the bag and add 1 cup wine. Add a little pepper and a few dashes of salt. Seal the bag and let the steaks marinate for several hours. Grill the steaks until they are done to your liking. Salt and pepper to taste. Then enjoy your dinner with a glass of the remaining wine and a buddy.

# Pepper Sirloin Steak

*Sirloin steak is often tender. If you don't have long to marinate this is a great cut to use. Flavors from spices and the grill will make it great.*

**2 top sirloin steaks, 2 inches
   thick**
**2 tablespoons black pepper**
**1 dash garlic powder**

**1 tablespoon coarse ground
   black pepper**
**1 dash salt**

Place steaks in a glass baking dish. Combine all of the spices and rub over the steaks pressing the spice into the meat. Flip the steak and do the other side. Cover with cling wrap for an hour or so while you get the fire going. Cook 'em how you like 'em.

# Dijon Mustard & Wine Sauce Steak

**4 beef tenderloin steaks,
   1 inch thick**
**2 tablespoons black pepper**
**1 teaspoon crushed red pepper**
**¼ cup dijon mustard**
**½ cup red wine**

**½ cup water**
**2 tablespoons chopped onion**
**1 teaspoon minced garlic**
**1 tablespoon salt**
**1 teaspoon flour**

Rub your steaks with the pepper and allow the steaks to rest. Combine the remaining ingredients (except flour) in a saucepan and simmer for about 10 minutes. Add in your flour and stir. Cook your steaks on the grill and top with the sauce. Serve hot.

# Grilled Steak and Tomatoes

2 T-bone steaks, 1-inch thick
Salt and pepper to taste
2 tablespoons steak sauce
3 tablespoons olive oil
1 teaspoon dried basil

½ teaspoon garlic powder
6 tomato slices, cut ¾-inch thick
2 tablespoons grated Parmesan
   cheese

Season your steaks with salt and pepper, brush with steak sauce. Cover and chill. Combine oil, basil and garlic powder and save for later. Place steaks on grill over medium coals. Season with salt and pepper as needed. Brush the basil sauce onto the tomatoes. About five minutes before steaks are done, place tomatoes on the grill with steaks; grill 2 to 3 minutes. Turn tomatoes over; sprinkle with Parmesan cheese before removing from grill.

## JAKE SAYS —

I love beef! Choice cuts are fillets, tenderloins, sirloin, strips, T-bone, and porterhouse. The less tender cuts include round, tips and flanks.

# Southwest Grilled
# Beer Steaks and Veggies

*This recipe makes a cheaper steak perfect for an entrée; or add it sliced to a tossed salad. You can even thin-cut it for great fajitas.*

3 pounds beef round steak
1 can Mexican or dark beer
½ cup salsa
1 onion, sliced not chopped
1 green bell pepper, sliced
1 red bell pepper, sliced

2 tablespoons minced garlic
2 tablespoons lime juice
1 tablespoon chopped cilantro
2 teaspoons red pepper
  seasoning
1 teaspoon salt

Place steaks in a glass baking dish. Combine beer, salsa, onions, red and green bell peppers, garlic, lime juice, cilantro, red pepper flakes and salt. Pour marinade over steaks. Cover and refrigerate overnight if possible. Remove the veggies from the marinade; wrap veggies in a foil pouch and place on grill over medium-high heat. Cook for about 10 minutes before adding the steaks to the grill. When done, remove steaks from grill and top with the vegetables.

# Cheap Beer Steaks

*Sometimes you just buy a couple of cheap steaks! And when you do, try this beer-based marinade.*

A couple of cheap steaks
1 can beer
½ cup French dressing
1 tablespoon garlic powder

1 tablespoon salt
1 tablespoon sugar
1 tablespoon lemon juice

Place the cheap steaks in a freezer bag and close. Bang the heck out of them with a blunt meat tenderizer or a heavy spoon. Pour in the beer and the remaining ingredients and seal the bag. Place the bag (zip top facing up) in the refrigerator and leave overnight or as long as possible. Cook over direct heat.

# Barbecue Beef Chuck Steak

1 well-trimmed beef chuck
   7-bone steak, cut ¾- to
   1-inch thick
1 cup finely chopped onion
1 cup ketchup

⅓ cup packed brown sugar
⅓ cup red wine vinegar
1 tablespoon Worcestershire
¼ teaspoon crushed red
   pepper

Combine all ingredients (except steak) in medium bowl to make a marinade. Place steak in 1 cup marinade, cover tightly and marinate in refrigerator 6 hours or as long as overnight, turning occasionally. Cover and refrigerate remaining marinade separately. Remove steak from marinade; discard marinade. Place steak on grid over medium, ash-covered coals. Grill, uncovered, 15 to 18 minutes for medium rare to medium doneness, turning occasionally.

# Rolled Steak with Veggies

*This is a neat recipe for a shank steak. Just flatten your steak as thin as possible, fill with the veggies, etc and roll up.*

1 shank or skirt steak
¼ cup olive oil
4 ounces cream cheese,
   softened
2 carrots, sliced length wise
1 cup onion slices
2 cups squash cut length wise

1 tablespoon garlic powder
1 teaspoon thyme
1 tablespoon parsley
1 tablespoon salt
1 tablespoon pepper
3 slices provolone cheese
½ cup steak sauce (your favorite)

Ask your butcher for the largest and thinnest cut of beef possible. You want something about 12-by-12-inches wide and about _-inch thick or so. Lay the steak out on a cookie sheet and brush with a bit of olive oil. Spread cream cheese over steak, add carrots, onions, squash, garlic, thyme, parsley, salt, pepper and provolone cheese. Gently roll the entire steak and either wrap with cooking string or secure with skewers. Baste the steak roll with your steak sauce and grill over high heat to brown (sear) edges. Wrap in foil and continue to cook for about 20 more minutes over medium heat. Turn often. Remove, unwrap and slice carefully to keep the shape.

# Hot Steak with Pepper Cheese Sauce

1½ pounds sirloin steak, 1-inch thick
1 (7-ounce) jar roasted red peppers
¾ teaspoon garlic salt
½ cup shredded jalapeño cheese
1 teaspoon butter
1 teaspoon milk

Place your steaks in a baking dish and add the jar of peppers. Cover and marinate as long as possible. Grill your steaks how you like them. Cook the peppers in a foil pack along side the steaks. In a small saucepan combine the garlic salt, cheese, butter and milk. Cook on low heat until you have a thick sauce and drizzle over the steaks topped with the peppers.

# Hawaii Seared Pineapple Steaks

4 top sirloin steaks
1 cup pineapple juice
½ cup soy sauce
¼ cup whiskey
1 tablespoon ginger
Salt and pepper to taste

Mix all except for salt and pepper and marinate steaks overnight. Remove steaks from marinade; salt and pepper the steaks. Cook quickly over high heat to sear in flavor.

So what makes a great steak? First the cut. Working muscle is tougher than cuts from other sections. I like my steaks cut thick, because it allows for more circulation of moisture or juice. The thinner the steak cut, the tougher it may get during cooking. Also buy as fresh as possible. And last but not least, a great steak can be simply seasoned with a bit of salt, pepper and butter, or seasoned for days in your secret steak seasoning or marinade.

# Short Sugar's Bar-B-Que

**2215 Riverside Drive • Danville, Virginia 24540**
**(434) 793-4800**

**234 S. Scales Street • Reidsville, North Carolina 27320**
**(336) 349-9128**

**1328 S. Scales Street • Reidsville, North Carolina 27320**
**(336) 342-7487**

After World War II, three friends started a restaurant. After one of them died in a car wreck, the remaining two—being family as well as friends and war buddies—decided to rename their restaurant after him. "His nickname was Short Sugar," present day owner Donnie Jones said. "His friends and family knew the way to honor their fallen comrade was to name their restaurant after him."

For over 52 years Short Sugar's has been serving Southern Virginia and people living in North Carolina the "Best BBQ around." Donnie told me that the original Short Sugar's was located in Reidsville, North Carolina. "That is the style of barbecue we serve. Our sauce is the original sauce that Short Sugar came up with over 52 years ago."

Even though Donnie is removed by years from the original founding members of Short Sugar's, he is still carrying the barbecue banner. "We have tried a few new things but it all comes back to the tried and true. We still cook over the same style barbecue pit using seasoned hickory wood just like they did over 52 years ago."

**NEAT THING:** Even though Short Sugar's now seats over 160 people and has a newly remolded dinning room, it still holds onto the past. Check out the paintings and memorabilia from Short Sugar's smoky years.

# Honey Grilled Flank Steaks

*My brothers taught me a valuable lesson early in life when it comes to hiking around the Smoky Mountains. One time after an Appalachian Trail trip, my brother Scot and a few of his buddies bought some cheap flank steaks the size of large platters. Each hiker maybe spent two bucks on these steaks and in an effort to save more money they used the foam container as plates. Of course they washed them. But I will always remember the lesson, even a cheap steak can taste great. With that in mind here is a nice recipe for some grilled flank steaks.*

**A couple of cheap steaks**          **1 teaspoon cumin powder**
**2 tablespoons honey**               **Splash of soy sauce**
**2 tablespoons lime juice**          **Salt and pepper to taste**

Tenderize your steaks and marinate them with the mixed ingredients in a zip-top bag. Grill them till ya like them!


# Stuffed Grilled Steak

*This recipe makes a great dish with the steak as the bun or tortilla shell.*

**2 palm-sized flank steaks**         **Salt and pepper to taste**
**Worcestershire sauce**              **1 cup mixed frozen vegetables**
**2 tablespoons allspice**            **1 cup shredded mozzarella**
**1 teaspoon garlic powder**          **cheese**

Pound steaks to thin them to about the width of a small tortilla shell. Brush with Worcestershire Sauce and sprinkle with allspice, garlic, salt and pepper. Thaw your veggies and gently sprinkle with allspice and a few drops of Worcestershire sauce. Cook the veggies covered in a microwave. Grill your steaks quickly on one side and turn. Spoon some veggies and cheese onto one side of the steak. Fold steak over and allow the cheese to melt. Serve hot.

# Pan Fried Sesame Steak

¼ cup chicken broth
2 tablespoons soy sauce
2 tablespoons brown sugar
1 tablespoon white sugar

1 tablespoon salt
1 tablespoon sugar
1 tablespoon sesame seeds
2 steaks of your choice

I would use a tender cut of steak but this recipe tastes great with any cut of beef. Combine all ingredients except the sesame seeds and the steaks. Stir well. Pour over steaks in a glass bowl and cover with cling wrap. Heat your skillet to medium-high heat) with a bit of olive oil if desired). Place your marinated steaks into the skillet and brown each side. Add in some remaining marinade. Top with seeds and continue to cook to your desired doneness and serve.

# Asian Barbecue London Broil

*This London Broil recipe is pretty easy. Many people seem to be scared to even try a London Broil. When ya tell them to just ask for a 2-inch round or flank steak they ease up a bit. The key here is two inches thick or more.*

2 pounds London Broil or top
 round steak or flank steak
⅓ teaspoon powdered ginger
⅓ cup red wine
⅓ cup pineapple juice

½ cup soy sauce
2 tablespoons brown sugar
1 small onion, minced
1 clove garlic, minced
1 teaspoon pepper

Mix all of the ingredients except for the meat in a large glass dish. Place the London Broil in the dish, cover and chill in the fridge for several hours. Turn the meat over at least once to marinate both sides. Place the London broil in a pan with a bit of oil and quickly brown all sides. Remove the meat and place on the grill and cook to an internal temperature of 140°. Baste often and turn. Remove from heat and allow to set for at least 5 minutes before serving.

# Steak on a Stick

*Perfect for flank steaks. Lots of flavor and a perfect finger food.*

2 to 3 pounds shank steak
½ cup Worcestershire sauce
¼ cup soy sauce
1 tablespoon vinegar

1 tablespoon of ginger
1 teaspoon brown sugar
Wood skewers as needed

Pound your steak so that it is very thin and tender. Slice into inch-wide strips about 5 inches long or so. Mix everything and marinate the meat for one hour or more. Place on a skewer like a wavy ribbon and grill. As soon as you remove from your heat source try topping with a dash of cajun seasoning or allspice.

# Smoked Beef Kabobs

*I like to use double-prong skewers for kabobs. But the toss-away wood skewers are fine as well.*

1 pound beef stew meat
2 tablespoons vegetable oil
1 tablespoon lemon or lime
   juice
1 tablespoon water
2 teaspoons Dijon mustard
1 teaspoon honey

½ teaspoon dried oregano
   leaves
¼ teaspoon crushed red pepper
1 green (or red or yellow) bell
   pepper, cut into 1-inch pieces
8 large mushrooms, washed

Combine and whisk together oil, lemon juice, water, mustard, honey, oregano and pepper in large bowl; add beef, bell pepper and mushrooms, stirring to coat. Place the ingredients on the skewers by threading pieces of beef, bell pepper and mushrooms on each of 4 (12-inch) skewers. Place your kabobs on the smoker. I like hickory wood. You can also place on the grill or bake in a roasting pan in the oven.

Cooking time for a smoker could be well over an hour or more. The grill using medium-high heat would take about 15 minutes. In the oven using the broiler with the pan low in the oven would take about 20 minutes.

# Mark's Mountain BBQ

**1435 North Kentucky 11 • Campton, Kentucky 41301**
**(606) 668-6613**

Located next to Natural Bridge State Park and Daniel Boone National Forest, the scenic area of Torrent Falls makes Mark's Mountain Barbecue a great place for food as well as a great place to catch up on some local history. Before the current bed and breakfast was in place, a resort dating back to the 1900s occupied the area.

Today, Mark's offers barbecue made in the great tradition of many 'que masters— "slow smoked food." According to the crew at Mark's, the area offers up some great wood for the smoking process including hickory and apple to name a few. Starting off with great ingredients also ensures great success. They proudly proclaim only using the freshest meats and veggies on the market.

Another great feature of Mark's Mountain BBQ is the location. Heck, it's in the mountains of Kentucky, removed from the busy day-to-day worries of everyday life. So when you visit, take a minute to soak in the local scenic views and wildlife. According to Mark, he would have it no other way! Before you get to Mark's, I bet you can smell the hickory aroma as it sifts through the mountains and valleys. You will be hungry before you get out of the car!

**GREAT EATS:** Mark's offers everything from pulled pork sandwiches to ribs and steaks. Their veggie burger is also popular.

**NEAT THING:** Mark's is located in a very cool and scenic place. Check out the three massive waterfalls and rock climbing opportunities available for climbers of all skill levels.

# Smoked Beef Tips

*This is a nice recipe using marinated beef chunks, veggies, and the flavor of hickory.*

2 pounds beef chunks (thick
   stew meat)
½ cup steak sauce
½ cup Italian dressing
1 tablespoon lemon juice
1 cup chopped squash

½ cup onion slices
1 potato, diced
1 teaspoon cumin powder
1 teaspoon garlic powder
¼ cup butter, softened

Marinate the meat in the steak sauce, Italian dressing and lemon juice. In a foil pan combine the marinated meat with the marinade sauce, all of the veggies, the cumin powder, garlic and butter. Lightly cover with foil and cook in a medium heat smoker. Baste with the juice in the bottom of the pan. Stir everything up to make sure it cooks evenly.

# Smoked Beef, Onion and Garlic

*This recipe has only three main ingredients but packs lots of flavor.*

1 pound stew-cut beef
2 garlic bulbs
2 large onions, chopped

2 tablespoons olive oil
2 teaspoons allspice

This is so simple. Rinse your steak. Peel your garlic to the cloves. Place everything in a zip-close bag and allow to marinate in the fridge. Pour into a foil pan and lightly cover with foil. Place in your smoker and close the lid. The cook time on this depends on the thickness of your steak cubes. Stir often, serve hot.

# Barbecued Beef Brisket

*The beef brisket is king of the beef barbecue world. This simple recipe is easy to follow and requires few ingredients. The hardest part is being able to wait it out. The secret to any good brisket, or barbecue for that matter, is to let it cook low and slow. You can set up a smoker for indirect heat or set up your covered grill for indirect heat and use soaked wood chips. Use what ya got!*

| | |
|---|---|
| 1 brisket, 6 pounds or so | 1 teaspoon salt |
| 1 tablespoon vegetable oil | 1 teaspoon black pepper |
| ¼ cup brown sugar | ½ teaspoon crushed red pepper |
| 2 tablespoons chili powder | 1 can beer |
| 2 tablespoons minced garlic | 2 tablespoons maple syrup |
| 2 tablespoons onion powder | 1 dash each black pepper, salt, |
| 1 teaspoon cumin powder | and garlic powder |

Take your brisket and wash it under cool water. This not only cleans the brisket but it also adds some extra moisture. Pat the brisket lightly with a paper towel. Take the tablespoon of oil and rub it into the brisket. Combine all of your dry ingredients (except the 1 dash each of black pepper, salt, and garlic powder) in a bowl to make a rub. Then rub the entire bowl of rub into the meat firmly. Next, wrap the brisket up as tight as possible in cling wrap. Store the wrapped brisket in the fridge—overnight if possible.

Prepare your smoker or covered grill for indirect heat. Place your brisket, with the fat side facing up, in a foil pan. Combine your beer, syrup, dashes of salt, pepper and garlic in a bowl and brush or mop the sauce over the brisket. Do this as lightly as possible so you will

## SMOKE NOTE

When barbecuing a brisket, turn at least once, and mop or brush with sauce every time you open the cover. Briskets take at least four to five hours to cook, depending on size, so be sure to have enough wood chips on hand if using a covered grill—and don't forget to soak your chips or wood chunks.

*(Barbecued Beef Brisket continued)*

not remove too much of the dry rub. Place your brisket on the smoker or covered grill and close the lid.

Here comes the hard part, let it cook. Check the brisket ONCE about every hour and mop or brush with more sauce. Towards the end of the cooking you may need to cover burning edges with light pieces of foil. When your brisket has an internal temp of about 190° (take the temp in the thickest part of the meat), remove your brisket and allow it to rest for a few minutes to allow the juices to settle. Slice and serve with some of the juice from the pan that has been boiled and strained. Hopefully you will have a nice smoke ring.

## Deck Chef Tip!

### So, What is a Smoke Ring?

A smoke ring is the pinkish ring inside smoked meat. If you smoke a beef brisket and slice it, hopefully you will have a dark outer crust, a lighter almost pinkish ring, then darker cooked meat. A smoke ring happens most often in beef. Many barbecue novice-type folk mistake this for under cooking. A smoke ring is caused by the natural chemicals in beef muscle tissue compared to that in pork and chicken. These chemicals break down during the slow heating process and keep this thin inner layer, about 1/8- to 1/2-inch thick ring, lighter in color even though it is completely cooked.

# Sweet 'n' Easy Barbecue Beef Ribs

1 tablespoon garlic powder
1 tablespoon pepper
1 tablespoon salt
1 tablespoon brown sugar
5 pounds (or more) country-
   style beef ribs

½ cup chopped onion
½ cup ketchup
½ cup strawberry jelly
¼ cup beer
¼ cup whiskey
¼ cup real butter

Combine the garlic, pepper, salt and sugar in a bowl. Rub this mix into the ribs. Place ribs in a covered dish or freezer bag and place in the fridge overnight. Combine the remaining ingredients and brush on the ribs. Grill or smoke over medium indirect heat for about 2 hours. Increase to medium to high heat and grill while basting. Serve hot.

# Smoked Corned Beef

*Back in the day (that's Southern Appalachian talk), corned beef and cabbage was a dish served in Ireland. The traditional process of making corned beef is about a 6- to 7-day event. Today I like to buy prepared corned beef from the store and smoke it or grill it. But if you want to give it a try here is how you do it. Corning is just another word for curing. There is no corn involved in the process.*

1 pound kosher salt
2 gallons water
8 pounds beef brisket
6 bay leaves

8 black peppercorns
1 onion, chopped
1 tablespoon salt
1 tablespoon black pepper

What you are doing is making a brine. Combine the water and the salt in a large pan. Submerge the meat completely. Place in the fridge for 6 days. On the seventh day remove and rinse the meat and place in clean water. Add the remaining ingredients and bring everything to a boil. Reduce the heat to medium and simmer for about an hour. Remove from the water and place on the smoker for about 2 hours. Your internal temperature should be 160°. You can serve with cooked cabbage, onions, carrots, potatoes and peppers. I have even had a corned beef that was blackened on the grill just before serving.

# Barbecue Steak Sandwich

*This is a great idea for some cheap cuts of beef.*

**A couple of cheap steaks**
**1 cup barbecue sauce**
  **(your favorite)**

**French rolls**
**Your favorite cheese**

Place your steaks on a safe cutting board and bang the daylights out of the steak with a tenderizer. Slice the steaks into thin slices and place on the grill or pan cook with a bit of oil. Once the meat starts to brown, coat with the barbecue sauce. Place on a French roll, top with cheese and serve hot.

# Easy Barbecue Po-Boy Sandwich

A good po-boy sandwich is hard to find. If you don't have time to round up some shrimp, try this version with some left-over barbecue. Take a French bun and cut like a hot dog bun. Lay a piece of Swiss cheese on both sides of the bun. Put in your barbecue. Fold over, wrap in foil heat and serve to your guests with toppings on the side.

## SMOKE NOTE

The tissue of beef is a bit different from pork. Beef barbecue, according to many pit masters, does not require the longer slow cooking hours of pork. This is because the long, slow and low methods with pork are designed to break down the connective tissue in the meat to make it tender. Beef barbecue can achieve the same tenderness with shorter cooking times. This is also why pork is often pulled or shredded while many beef barbecue recipes are chopped or sliced.

# Gary's Jerky Stand

### Sand Rock, Alabama

So here I am driving down a country road in Sand Rock, Alabama, on the way to Centre, Alabama, when out of the corner of my eye I see a small sign that says "JERKY" in big letters. As I drive I see a few more signs and I decide that I need some jerky!

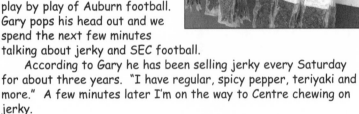

Just as I come around a bend I hit the brakes at the last sign and pull off the side of the road up to a trailer. Coming from the trailer I can hear the play by play of Auburn football. Gary pops his head out and we spend the next few minutes talking about jerky and SEC football.

According to Gary he has been selling jerky every Saturday for about three years. "I have regular, spicy pepper, teriyaki and more." A few minutes later I'm on the way to Centre chewing on jerky.

**Beef jerky has roots that go way back.** I talked to a guy in Cherokee, North Carolina, that was selling jerky, and he told me Native Americans have been making jerky since "the sun began to shine." Of course this led to about 30 questions about jerky. Seems the word comes from an old Native American word that the Spanish could not pronounce, and then American settlers pronounced it even worse. Now we call it jerky.

I have also heard several people refer to jerky as strip jerk which would indicate roots to Africa. Wherever it came from, the reasons are the same for making and eating jerky. In the old days, settlers used the semi-dried, cured and more than often, smoked, strips of meat as a source of protein and as a food staple. It came in handy for long trips or when times were lean. Native Americans knew this, settlers and mountain men knew this, armies during the Civil War knew this, and today hikers, campers and more know that a small amount of jerky goes a long way.

# Mediterranean Beef Roast

½ cup fresh lemon juice
2 tablespoons fresh lime juice
⅓ cup red wine vinegar
2 cloves garlic, finely chopped
2 tablespoons finely chopped
  oregano

½ teaspoon salt
½ teaspoon pepper
1 cup olive oil
2- or 3-pound beef roast

Make your marinade first by combining all ingredients (except oil and roast) in blender and blend well. Place your roast in a glass baking dish and pour marinade over. Cover with cling wrap and refrigerate overnight if possible. You can grill this roast or smoke it. Use your remaining marinade to brush over the roast as it cooks.

# Country Beef Pot Roast

3- to 4-pound boneless chuck roast
2 cups water
2 beef bullion cubes
½ cup wine vinegar
3 cloves garlic, crushed
1 onion, chopped
¼ cup mustard

2 tablespoons Worcestershire sauce
2 teaspoons dried thyme
6 potatoes, cubed
1 pound carrots, sliced
1 pound trimmed green beans
1½ tablespoons flour
½ cup water

In a small saucepan mix water and bullion cubes. Simmer until bullion cube dissolves. Add vinegar, garlic, onion, mustard, Worcestershire sauce and thyme. Stir, turn off heat and let rest. Place roast in glass baking dish and add potatoes, carrots and beans. Bake in a 350° oven, basting often. When done add the ½ cup water, flour and drippings into a small saucepan and simmer for about 5 minutes. Stir until thick. Serve gravy over roast or in a gravy boat.

# Barbecue Beef Roast

*This beef barbecue is much like a pork roast. But many cuts of beef roast may not have as much fat. This is why you need to wrap the roast... well, you'll see in the recipe.*

1 beef roast, about 4 pounds
2 tablespoons garlic powder
2 tablespoons paprika
2 tablespoons black pepper
1 tablespoon salt

½ cup mustard
¼ cup vinegar
¼ cup vegetable oil
¼ cup barbecue sauce
  (your favorite)

Combine your garlic, paprika, black pepper and salt for your rub. Gently rub into the roast. Wrap your roast in cling wrap and store in fridge overnight. Remove your meat and baste with the mustard and vinegar. Place on the smoker with hickory and smoke to an internal temp of 150°. Remove from smoker and rub with vegetable oil and barbecue sauce. Wrap very tight in several layers of foil and place back in a high temperature smoker or even on a grill to finish the cooking process. If you finish cooking on a grill directly over the heat source make sure to turn often to avoid burning the edges. You can shred, pull, chop or slice this beef barbecue.

# Deck Chef Tip!

## Pot Roast with a Twist

You can cook a roast on a covered grill. Combine everything in a disposable foil pan, lightly cover with foil, and toss some wood chips in with the charcoal. Make sure you baste often and enjoy the smoky flavor. Next time you make a roast try these little tips.

- Try using a dry rub on your roast. Salt, pepper, garlic and a bit of sugar is the easy way to go.

- Cut a few deep slices in your roast and insert something extra like jalapeños, garlic cloves or any spice of your choice.

- When you place your roast in the pan, add Worcestershire sauce, a bit of pineapple juice or maybe a few tablespoons of flavored, brewed, coffee. When you have everything ready to go, add a bit of extra water, cover well and cook.

- Turn the roast over for the last 15 or so minutes of cooking time. This will allow the top part of the roast to soak up some juice so it will be tender throughout. When you serve the roast, just turn it over again to present the best side to your guests.

- Go ahead and add those carrots and potatoes but also try some blackened peppers, banana peppers, onions, squash or whatever you have in the fridge!

# Red Wine & Garlic Beef Roast

5- to 6-pound beef roast
1 cup red wine
½ cup oil1 tablespoon apple
  cider vinegar
2 cloves garlic, minced

¼ cup minced onion
¼ cup Worcestershire sauce
1 teaspoon salt
1 teaspoon pepper

Combine all ingredients and marinate the roast for about 3 or 4 hours turning and basting. Place in a shallow pan with some of the marinade and cook in a smoker set up for medium-high heat. If using a covered grill with wood chips, use indirect heat. Boil the remaining marinade and use as a basting sauce. Cook to an internal temperature of 160° to 170°. Remove from heat, cover and let rest for 5 minutes before serving.

# Easy Country Roast

*Want a roast that's full of flavor but easy to make? Here it is. You can cook it on the smoker or in the oven.*

1 (4-pound) roast

**GLAZE:**
¼ cup pineapple juice
¼ cup soy sauce

2 tablespoons brown sugar
1 teaspoon flour

Combine glaze ingredients in a 1-cup glass measure, mixing well. Microwave on HIGH 2½ to 3 minutes. Place the roast in a deep foil pan. Poke several holes in the roast with a fork and place the glaze over the roast. Lightly cover with foil and place on your smoker or covered grill with high heat. For the oven, cover and bake at about 350° for about 2–3 hours. Baste often as needed.

# As Basic as Possible Burgers

1 pound ground beef
1 tablespoon minced garlic
1 tablespoon hot sauce

1 tablespoon taco sauce
¼ cup fine minced onion

Combine all ingredients, form your patties, chill in fridge to set shape. Grill 'em how you like 'em!

**VARIATION:**

To make Barbecue Sauce Burgers, leave out the hot sauce and taco sauce. Add 3 tablespoons barbecue sauce.

# Hot as Heck Burgers

1 pound ground beef
1 tablespoon hot sauce
1 tablespoon crushed red
  pepper

1 (4.5-ounce) can green chilies
1 teaspoon Cajun seasoning
1 teaspoon prepared horseradish

Mix all together, form your patties and cook on the grill.

*My son Macee (pronounced Macy) is a firm believer that any hamburger is a good hamburger. According to Mace, the best part of having a Dad that writes cookbooks is getting to eat burgers and barbecue. The worst part is that, "Dad has to take a picture of everything he cooks!"*

# Stuffed Cheese Burgers

1 pound ground beef
1 tablespoon butter, softened
1 teaspoon garlic powder
1 teaspoon parsley

1 teaspoon allspice
Several slices of your
   favorite cheese

Make equal amounts of very thin hamburger patties. Combine butter, garlic, parsley and allspice. Mix well into a seasoned butter. Spread some seasoned butter onto half of the patties. Place a slice of cheese on the patty making sure it does not overreach the edge. (If you make 8 thin burgers, you will need 4 slices of cheese, 6 patties means you need 3 slices of cheese, etc.) Just break any overhanging bits off and layer it on top of the cheese. Place another patty over the patty with butter and cheese and press the edges together firmly. Chill to set the shape. Cook them on the grill, toss 'em on a bun with your favorite toppings, and enjoy.

*If you are ever in Chickamauga, Georgia, look up living historian John Culpepper. He can tell you how our forefathers cooked "back in the day." John is full of great stories.*

# SUPER Cheese Burgers

*If you like meatballs, then the flavor of this burger will knock you down.*

Take your hamburger meat and add some shredded cheese of your choice. Try something besides Cheddar. Add some minced garlic, a few dashes of olive oil and some Italian seasoning. Form your burgers and fire up the grill.

# Hawaiian Pineapple Burgers

**1 pound ground beef**
**1 can crushed pineapple**
**1 teaspoon ginger**
**1 tablespoon brown sugar**
**1 dash garlic powder**

Drain juice from pineapple into a separate bowl. (You'll use this as a grilling baste while you cook.) Mix all ingredients, form patties, cook, and baste with the pineapple juice.

# Mini Meat Loafs

**1 pound ground beef**
**1 tablespoon butter, softened**
**½ cup cracker crumbs**
**1 egg**
**½ cup salsa**
**¼ cup chopped onion**
**1 teaspoon garlic powder**
**1 teaspoon parsley**
**1 cup tomato soup**

Mix all together except the soup. If need to help keep form, add some extra cracker crumbs. Form 4 small meat loaves out of your mix, and cook on the grill or in the oven. Baste with the tomato soup. Top with some of your favorite veggies. I like onion, Cuban peppers, and bell peppers.

# The Bar-B-Que Place

**1502 Gault Avenue South • Fort Payne, Alabama 35967
(256) 845-6155**

After years of working in coal mines and as a police officer, Karl Hood decided to make a change and opened The Bar-B-Que Place. "Dad and Mom bought this restaurant back in 1984, and I have grown up here," said Karl's son Burt. The Bar-B-Que Place is a family business with everyone pitching in. "We work together," Burt said. Customers are often called by name, and stories are frequently swapped with drive-through customers.

While he gave me a quick tour of the smokehouse, Burt explained that things have not changed much since the beginning. "We still have the same basic menu. We still cook with hickory, we make our own sauce, and we cook as low and slow as possible," he said. "That's why people come back."

**GREAT EATS:** The menu is filled with great barbecue including pork, beef, and chicken. They also have a great side item called Jo Jo's — a hot plate of very thinly sliced potatoes that are seasoned, battered, and then deep-fried.

**NEAT THING:** I had a great chat with Burt. He said that anyone who wants to cook good barbecue needs to remember two things: "Low and slow" and "Learn more as you go!"

# Barbecue Burger

This is a neat idea for a burger. Make the burger mix of your choice. Cook the burger like you want. Before removing from the grill, top with leftover barbecue and your favorite cheese. Let the cheese melt, and serve on a bun with your favorite toppings. Nice and simple.

# Kent's BBQ Wrap

*This is an easy recipe that I make from leftover barbecue.*

1 (8-ounce) package fat-free cream cheese
1 cup shredded Cheddar cheese
½ cup chopped green onion
½ cup bacon bits
2 tablespoons Worcestershire sauce
1 tablespoon crushed red pepper
1 cup leftover barbecued pork or beef
8 flour tortillas

Combine all ingredients except the barbecue and the tortilla shells. Mix together well to make a butter-like paste. Spread the paste over the tortilla; add a few pieces of barbecue. Roll the tortilla up and cook in an oven with a cookie sheet, on the grill wrapped in foil for a few minutes, or in a skillet with a bit of butter.

# Barbecue Biscuits

*This is a pretty cool finger food that is perfect for a quick tailgate item. Plus it is perfect for kids to try. Cook and use some of your favorite sauce as a dipping sauce.*

½ cup leftover barbecued meat
¼ cup shredded jack cheese
1 can pre-made biscuits

Mix the barbecue and cheese. Open the can of biscuits and flatten them out a bit. Take a pinch of the mix and place it in the center of the flattened biscuit. Fold the biscuit over and press edges together to form a ball or wonton shape. Bake in oven at 350° for about ten minutes, or cook on covered grill with indirect heat until biscuits rise and turn golden brown.

# Marinated Hot Dogs

*While in Atlanta for a doctor appointment, I read an article in a magazine about a local restaurant that specializes in HOT hot dogs. I thought about nabbing the magazine but the receptionist kept an eye on me. I didn't want to be tackled at the door by the waiting room magazine police, so I just came home and tried my own recipe. The great thing about this recipe is that you can use any seasoning that you desire.*

**1 pack of all-beef, bun-size hot dogs**
**2 cups cold water**

**1 (3-ounce) bottle hot sauce**
**3 tablespoons steak sauce**

Use a fork and poke a few holes along the dogs. Don't do too many or the hot dog may fall apart when cooking. Place the hot dogs in a dish deep enough to hold them. Mix the remaining ingredients and pour over the dogs. Marinate as long as possible. Grill your dogs and serve hot!

# Barbecue Bologna

*Just when you think you have the whole barbecue thing figured out, you meet a guy with a recipe for barbecue bologna. David "Porky" Scott's restaurant in Woodbury, Tennessee, has tons of great food on the menu, but the item that sticks in my mind is the smoked barbecue bologna. It's easy to make, tastes great, and is definitely a conversation starter for your next cookout.*

**1 whole length bologna, not sliced**
**1 cup your favorite barbecue sauce**

**⅓ cup beer**
**1 tablespoon hot sauce**
**1 teaspoon garlic powder**

Take the bologna and make 3- to 4¼-inch deep cuts along the length of the bologna. NOT SLICES. Mix the remaining ingredients and marinate the bologna as long as possible. I did mine overnight. Remove the bologna and place it on the smoker or covered grill with wood chips using medium-high indirect heat. Cook until the bologna plumps. Baste often with remaining sauce and turn when needed. Slice and serve hot.

# Pork

**I think I was about 18 years old** before somebody asked me if I wanted pork or beef barbecue. Growing up in the South, I did not even know there were different types of barbecue. I just thought its was all . . . barbecue! WELL, by golly, I know that in some parts of the country, it's pork, baby. And then in some parts it's beef, lamb, chicken and even wild game. This section is dedicated to pork, pork barbecue, pork fat and maybe some pork. Read on, cook and enjoy!

# The Easy Way to Smoke a Pork Butt

*Smoking a pork butt is really pretty easy. Well, after I messed up a few, it is pretty easy. The basic lesson that I can pass onto future barbecue chefs is to take your time. Don't overcook, undercook, over spice or under spice. Just keep it simple and let the smoke do the work with this easy recipe.*

| | |
|---|---|
| 1 large pork butt | ½ cup brown sugar |
| 1 small can pineapple juice | ¼ cup lemon juice |
| ⅓ cup hot sauce | 2 tablespoons black pepper |
| ½ cup mustard | 1 tablespoon salt |

Place the pork butt in a glass bowl. Combine remaining ingredients and pour over the butt. Cover bowl well with cling wrap and place in fridge for about 6 hours. Set up your covered smoker for medium indirect heat at about 200 to 250°. Place butt in smoker and smoke to an internal temp of 190°. Depending on the size of the butt, this should take as few as 6 hours or more. Whenever you check your smoke, take a moment to baste with the marinade. Cover areas that might be burning with loose foil.

Pull pork using tongs and a fork. If the meat does not pull easily with the fork, rub down with the marinade, wrap in foil and place back over a higher heat for about 30 minutes. Remember, keep it simple. Get your smoke going, get your pork going, close the lid and leave it alone.

## Deck Chef Tip!

## The End is Near

Often when slow smoking a Boston Butt, the internal temperature reaches about 170 to 180 degrees and stops for a while. Many folk would throw more wood on the fire and end up burning a great piece of meat. Calm down and take a deep breath. What is happening is that much of the fat is beginning to render off. When this process is done, the internal temp will begin to rise to the 190-degree mark.

**Boston Butt is not really a butt at all.** The Boston Butt pork roast is actually a front shoulder pork roast. They are juicy and full of flavor, make great roasts and great barbecue. You can buy it bone-in or boneless, and keep an eye out for Boston Butt steak cuts. According to the folks at the National Pork Board, the name "Boston Butt" refers to the way Boston meat packers stored their meat. The shoulder roasts were cut and stored in barrels often called butts or casks. This way of cutting the meat and storing it became known as a Boston cut. Now we just call this cut of meat a Boston Butt.

# Carolina Pork Barbecue

*The key, according to my pit master friends, for good old Carolina Pork Barbecue is some good apple cider vinegar, lots of smoke, plenty of time, and a nice thin barbecue sauce to pour over it before you eat it! This is a simple recipe.*

**1 pork butt (shoulder)**
**¼ cup hot sauce**
**1 gallon cider vinegar**
**1 tablespoon crushed red pepper**
**1¼ cups Worcestershire sauce**

Place your pork butt in a deep bowl. Mix all remaining ingredients together and marinate the pork for several hours. Remove pork and boil marinade to use as a basting sauce for the meat. Cook the pork long and slow. Use indirect heat over a real wood fire, preferably hickory. Temperature should be around 220°, and it takes at least 1½ hours per pound, or until internal temperature reaches 180° to 190°. Pull with a fork and serve as quickly as possible.

# Jaguar XJ6 Smoker

## Built by John Worley • Memphis, Tennessee

So, I am walking with my buddy Bill Lawrence, Jr., head of concessions for the National Cornbread Festival in the Appalachian foothills of South Pittsburg, Tennessee, and he says, "You have to meet this guy." I follow Bill's six-foot frame through the crowd as he meets, greets and shakes hands with just about everyone he sees. "Here ya go!" Bill says, as he motions me towards a car with smoke pouring out of it.

Before me was the creation of John Worley—a 1978 Jaguar XJG that John and his friends turned into a barbecue smoker. Being a guy, the combination of a very cool car and barbecue was a bit of barbecue heaven. "This baby has 48,000 original miles on it and can hold about 500 pounds of meat," John told me.

Being in the automotive industry and loving barbecue, John thought combining the two would be a great way to promote business. It must be, because the same number of people that bought John's barbecue, stopped to take a look at and have their picture taken with John and the car.

"It is a lot of fun," John said. "People really seem to enjoy it, and it makes some great 'cue!" The car's engine has been replaced by a fire box, which doubles as a stove to cook beans on. The interior is a vast chamber complete with swing out trays packed with smaller cuts. Yep, you guessed right. The doors now have shelves attached that are perfect for a few small butts or birds.

# Spicy Pan Smoked Pork

*I tried this recipe after a friend and I ate at a Tex-mex restaurant. I asked the owner about the pork used in one dish and he gave me a quick tour of the cooking areas. The secret to his pork was that he turned a portion of his covered outside grill into a slow cooker by using a large foil pan. He mixed all of his ingredients, spices and all, in the pan, added the pork, placed the whole thing on the smoker, and lightly covered it with foil. The finished product was a spicy pork butt filled with smoked flavor served on a plate with Spanish fried rice, seasoned corn and tortilla chips. This is so easy!*

**2 medium-sized pork roasts**
**1 can tomato sauce**
**1 bottle barbecue sauce**
  **(your favorite)**
**1 cup white wine vinegar**
**1 onion, chopped**
**1 green pepper, chopped**

**1 hot chili pepper, chopped**
**1 hot banana pepper, chopped**
**1 tablespoon ginger**
**1 tablespoon chili powder**
**1 tablespoon brown sugar**
**1 teaspoon powdered cumin**
**½ cup chopped cilantro**

Mix together all ingredients, including the pork, in a foil pan large enough to hold all of it. Baste meat well and cover pan with foil. Place the pan in the smoker with medium indirect heat, and cook on low for about 6 to 8 hours or until pork is tender and has an internal temp of 190°. Take the finished pork out and chop it into small pieces. While you are doing this, boil some of the juice from the pan and add it to your finished meat to keep it tender until serving.

# Couch Potato Barbecue Pork Sandwich

*Everybody who loves barbecue knows that a good pulled pork barbecue sandwich is the result of a long day's work on somebody's part. If you just don't have the time to slow cook some pork . . . if you can't get to the smoker or grill because of knee-deep snow or tornadoes . . . here is a recipe that can hold you over until the smell of hickory can once again fill your neighborhood.*

1 (4-pound) pork roast
1 can beef broth
⅓ cup hot pepper sauce
⅓ cup Worcestershire sauce
½ cup ketchup
½ cup molasses or syrup

¼ cup yellow mustard
1 tablespoon apple cider vinegar
¼ cup chopped onion
1 teaspoon garlic powder
1 teaspoon crushed red pepper
1 teaspoon lemon juice

Take your pork butt and place it in the bottom of a large slow cooker (one of the neatest Christmas presents I ever got!). Combine beef broth, hot pepper sauce and Worcestershire sauce, and pour over pork. Cover and cook on HIGH for 5 hours. Check every hour and spoon juice over the meat. You may need

> ## JAKE SAYS —
> Even if you have to use a crockpot to cook barbecue, don't worry, you can still get some smoke flavor.

to turn the meat over. Cook to an internal temp of 200°.

Meanwhile, for sauce, combine remaining ingredients in a large saucepan and simmer about 10 minutes. Place cooked pork on a clean cutting board (make sure to save about ½ cup of the juice from the slow cooker). Chop or pull the pork and place it in the saucepan with the ½ cup of juice and sauce. Simmer 10 minutes, and serve hot with Texas toast or burger buns.

# Crock Pot Pulled Pork

*The crockpot is a neat thing. You can toss in some meat, some seasoning, some juice and let it go for several hours. This is great when 8 inches of snow is on the ground.*

| | |
|---|---|
| **1 pork roast** | **1 tablespoon sugar** |
| **Juice of 1 lemon** | **1 tablespoon brown sugar** |
| **1 small onion, chopped** | **1 bottle barbecue sauce** |

Place your pork roast in the crockpot and add all of your ingredients. You may need to add water, depending on the size of your crockpot. Cooking time can vary as well. A roast can take anywhere from 6 to 12 hours depending on the size of the roast, the heat setting, the size of the pot, the phase of the moon and more. When done, pour off water and pull meat into shredded pieces. Add a bit more of your favorite barbecue sauce, if needed.

## Deck Chef Tip!

### Crockpot Tip

To add some smoke flavor to your crockpot barbecue, pull cooked pork into small strips and place it on a covered grill with wood chips or wood pellets for an hour or so before serving. Keep it moist with some of the juice from the crockpot. It won't taste like it was smoked for 12 hours, but it will be pretty darned good.

# Cajun Pulled Pork

1 (4- to 6-pound) pork roast
1 tablespoon paprika
2½ teaspoons salt
1 teaspoon onion powder
1 teaspoon garlic powder

1 teaspoon cayenne
¾ teaspoon white pepper
¾ teaspoon black pepper
¾ teaspoon dried thyme
¾ teaspoon oregano

Mix all ingredients, except pork, and store in an airtight container. When ready to cook, rub roast with mixture. Prepare medium-hot fire and cook the pork over indirect heat. Depending on the size of your roast and temps the cooking time can take 4 to 7 hours, give or take a beer or two. Pull the pork, and if needed, add a few dashes of Cajun seasoning.

## Deck Chef Tip!

### How to Pull Pulled Pork

An easy way to tell if you have cooked your pork roast long enough is when you pull it. Pork cooked properly pulls very easily. It should fall apart or pull apart easily using sturdy kitchen forks. If you start pulling and it seems tough, quickly baste it in some oil, add a few spices, wrap it in several wraps of foil, and place the whole thing on a covered grill for several minutes, turning often. This will help render the connective tissue and break down the fats further so that you can pull it with ease.

# Hot Chili Pepper Pork Loin

*This is a very spicy way to do a pork tenderloin but still have tons of natural flavor.*

**1 boneless pork loin**
**½ cup apple vinegar**
**½ cup chili powder**
**1 tablespoon salt**
**1 tablespoon cumin powder**

**1 tablespoon sugar**
**½ cup chopped hot banana**
  **pepper**
**1 lemon slice**

Marinate loin in vinegar and cover with cling wrap. Place in fridge for about 4 hours. Combine all dry ingredients and the chopped banana peppers, and separate into two parts. Spread one part onto a flat dish and roll loin in rub. Make sure whole loin is covered with rub. Use a spoon (otherwise the pepper may irritate your skin) to press rub into meat. Place meat on medium-high heat and cook for about an hour, turning often. When loin reaches internal temp of about 130°, cover with the remaining rub. Continue to cook to internal temp of 170° and serve sliced. Squeeze a few drops of lemon over slices.

### SMOKER VARIATION

In the smoker, cook with indirect medium high heat. Your cooking time will be longer. I suggest using a bit of extra lemon juice in a water-filled drip pan.

*A couple heads into the legendary Armstrong's Barbecue in Summerville, Georgia, for a fantastic meal.*

# The Hickory Pit Bar-B-Que

**5611 Ringgold Road • East Ridge, Tennessee 37412**
**(423) 894-1217**

The city of East Ridge went without barbecue for a bit when All Star closed down and another restaurant closed and became a Mexican diner. But now Hickory Pit Bar-B-Que has a home in the old Chick's Building. Hickory Pit is run by Mike Ford and his crew of friendly faces, and sits just off Ringgold Road, or Highway 41. Just look for the catering truck with the huge pig painted on the side. During the summer months, the air is filled with hickory aroma and a massive inflatable chef with a pig.

When you visit Mike and his crew at Hickory Pit be ready for some downhome conversation with the pit master. When you order on a slow day, you can stand at the counter and discuss the fine art of barbecue, and other topics, with Mike.

**GREAT EATS:** Mike has a great menu that caters to 'que lovers as well as those who are craving a HUGE ground sirloin burger. Appetizers include deep fried broccoli called "Dynobites." Dishes include chopped plates, spare ribs, chicken, beef, pork and a great barbecue salad.

**NEAT THING:** He prepares all of your order in plain sight. That's pretty neat. You can also expect to be greeted with a big smile and a thoughtful thank you when you're done with your meal and headed for the door. According to Mike, that's just the way you do business.

# Mixed Fruit Stuffed Pork Tenderloin

*Combine fresh fruit, pork and smoke for a great dish. Fruit adds flavor to recipes that can be found no where else. So enjoy!*

⅓ cup chopped onion
1 clove garlic, minced
1 tablespoon melted margarine
½ cup red wine
1 small apple, peeled and
   chopped
1 small pear, peeled and
   chopped

¼ cup raisins
¾ teaspoons rosemary
¾ teaspoon thyme
¼ cup apple juice
2 tablespoons brown sugar
¼ cup croutons
Large dash of salt and pepper
1 whole pork tenderloin

Sauté onion and garlic in margarine in medium pan; stir in wine. Add in the apple, pear and raisins and cook for about 2 to 3 minutes. Add rosemary and thyme and cook over medium heat to reduce the wine. Add apple juice and brown sugar. Stir in croutons and salt and pepper to taste. With a sharp knife cut the tenderloin almost in half lengthwise. Rub the outside of the tenderloin with some salt and pepper and spoon fruit stuffing into the slit. Roast meat, uncovered, in preheated 350° oven until you get an internal temp of 160°. The cooking time in an oven will be about an hour or less. On the grill it could take over an hour and in a smoker the cooking process could take about 3 hours or more.

# Steve's Easy Vinegar & Mustard BBQ Pork

*"Tarheel" Steve from North Carolina is a tailgate freak. He loves going to football games and setting up camp. Here is his recipe for easy barbecue that's quick. He emailed this recipe after I met him at a barbecue restaurant.*

2 small pork roasts　　　　　½ cup brown sugar
1 cup vinegar　　　　　　　¼ cup black pepper and salt
1 cup mustard　　　　　　　combined

Take your roasts and butterfly them. Combine the remaining ingredients and rub into meat. Wrap in foil and cook in a conventional oven at 400° for several hours until done. Remove from foil and pull while hot. Place in a sealed container and save for game day. On game day Steve places the pulled meat in a foil pan and reheats on his portable smoker using lots of Hickory chips and a watered down vinegar BBQ sauce to keep meat moist. He then serves up great barbecue sandwiches on mini French bread loafs. Steve's tip for tailgaters is do as much at home in the kitchen as possible and reheat on the grill or smoker before the game.

# Gentleman Jack Pork

*This simple marinade is great on pork. I have used it as a marinade base, a sauce, and a finishing sauce, and every time it comes out great.*

1 pork tenderloin　　　　　　1 tablespoon minced garlic
½ cup Gentleman Jack whiskey　1 tablespoon onion powder
¼ cup melted butter　　　　　Cracked pepper
¼ cup honey　　　　　　　　Cloves

Combine all ingredients and place in a freezer bag to marinate meat for at least 4 hours. Brown the outside of the tenderloin in a skillet with some oil. Baste with remaining sauce and either smoke or grill. Slice and serve hot with fresh bread or Texas Toast.

**Note:** Gentleman Jack Rare Tennessee Whiskey is a higher-end whiskey produced by Jack Daniel Distillery. It has a smoother flavor than traditional Jack Daniels Old No. 7 Tennessee Whiskey, and is well worth the extra cost.

# Applesauce Pork Loin

*Applesauce is an amazing food. Not only can you eat it with a spoon, add it to oat-meal and more, you can also cook a great pork loin with it. Here is a method of cooking a big pile of barbecue using applesauce and some brown sugar.*

| | |
|---|---|
| 3 pounds center cut pork loin | 8 peppercorns |
| 1 tablespoon sage | 1 tablespoon seasoned salt |
| 1 teaspoon allspice | 1 cup applesauce |
| 1 teaspoon nutmeg | ½ cup brown sugar |

Set up your grill for roasting with a drip pan. This can be done with a pan directly under the meat, and coals placed on either side of pan.

Combine sage, allspice, nutmeg, peppercorns and seasoned salt. Pat the pork loin dry and press spices onto roast. Roast in a covered grill at about 320° until internal temperature of 160°. Roasting time should be about 90 minutes. During the last 30 minutes of roasting, combine applesauce and brown sugar, and coat top of loin (reserving some to re-coat the loin periodically). Continue roasting until internal temperature is 190°, occasionally adding more applesauce mixture to the top. Allow loin to cook for another 20 minutes or so after you apply the last of the applesauce mixture. Carve into thin slices and serve hot.

## THE PIGGY GETS WIGGLY

**In 1916 a man named Clarence Saunders** had a neat idea. Put food and goods on the shelves where people could reach them. Mr. Saunders pioneered the modern day grocery store and named it after pork. Nobody really knows why he named it after pigs. But if you are going to sell food to Southern folk, then having a pig in your store logo ain't that silly! According to Piggly Wiggly® home office, the first Piggly Wiggly, opened in Memphis, Tennessee, in 1916.

# Appalachian Wine-Fried Pork

*Many people that I have talked to after a visit to the Southern Appalachian Mountains are surprised about the number of wineries located in this area. Of course, any self-respecting deck chef would have to stop by and pick up a few bottles . . . for cooking purposes, of course. Here is a neat recipe that uses a dry red wine combined with butter and some black pepper. I cooked it in a seasoned iron skillet on the burner side of my gas grill. If you don't have a burner on your grill or an iron skillet, just head to the kitchen.*

1 large pork tenderloin
1 tablespoon black pepper
4 tablespoons melted butter
⅔ cup plus ½ cup red wine,
   divided
⅓ cup plus 3 tablespoons
   water, divided

⅛ teaspoon basil
1 teaspoon minced garlic
¼ cup white flour
Fresh ground black pepper
   to taste

Rub the pork tenderloin with pepper. Melt butter in your skillet. Place your tenderloin in the skillet, and brown on all sides. Remove the skillet from the heat and let cool for a few minutes. Slowly, and carefully, add ⅔ cup wine, ⅓ cup water, and basil. Simmer for about 20 minutes on all sides. Remove the tenderloin from the skillet and add ½ cup wine, garlic, 3 tablespoons water and flour. Stir into a sauce and spoon over the tenderloin. Top with fresh ground black pepper to taste.

# Sorghum & Pepper Pork Loin

*Sorghum is a natural sweetener that is legendary in the South. While you may not find it in your local grocery store, many roadside fruit and veggie stands have it.*

1 (2–3 pound) boneless
  pork loin
2 tablespoons salt
½ cup sorghum syrup
¼ cup cranberry juice

¼ cup lemon lime soda
1 tablespoon thyme
½ teaspoon garlic powder
Salt and pepper to taste

With a sharp knife, score an X pattern on top of loin. Place in a large bowl and cover with water. Add 2 tablespoons salt and let soak overnight, if possible. Combine remaining ingredients and pour over loin. Rub all over to make sure all sides are coated. Cover and store in fridge for at least an hour or two. Remove and sprinkle with salt and pepper. Set up smoker or grill for medium to high heat of about 300°. Remove loin from dish and wrap in foil tightly and place in smoker/grill. Cook for 1 hour. Fold back foil to expose scored side and baste with remaining sauce. Let brown as you continue to baste with remaining sauce. Cook to an internal temp of 190°.

## Deck Chef Tip!

### Is It Ready Yet?

The National Pork Board and the USDA suggest that pork is best when cooked to medium doneness or an internal temperature of 160 degrees. Use a meat thermometer to judge doneness. The reason many pit masters look for a higher temperature is to make sure that more of the fat is cooked off, offering a finished product that is easier to pull. When cooking a roast, remove from the oven when the internal temperature reaches 155 degrees, and allow the roast to stand for 10 minutes before slicing. The roast's internal temperature will rise about five degrees after removing from the oven.

# Three Wise Men

## Jim Reynolds, Wally Witkowski and Coach McCarthy

*Jim Reynolds (left) and Wally Witkowski.*

**W**hen the idea of making a cook-book came up, the three people I talked to first were Jim Reynolds, Wally Witkowski, and Coach Mack McCarthy.

Jim, J. R. for short, has been the radio voice of the University of Tennessee at Chattanooga for over 24 years. What does the voice of the UTC Mocs look for in a hot wing? "A wing hot enough to make you remember it the next day is a good wing!"

Wally is a great friend who co-hosts the Village Idiots radio show with J. R. on WGOW radio in Chattanooga. Wally is famous around town for his outspoken views on all kinds of social issues, but his other claim to fame is that he knows almost every restaurant owner in a 100-mile radius of Chattanooga. So, what is Wally's secret for the perfect southern-style meal? "Friends, family, and fun!"

Mack McCarthy is well known around basketball circles. In less than 10 years, he's coached teams to 309 wins (177 losses) appearing in five NCAA basketball tournaments, taking teams to seven post-season appearances, eight conference championships, and five conference tournament championships. Coach Mack loves to talk sports, but he'll also talk about barbecue ANYTIME! He firmly believes in the combination of great barbecue, good people, and a few old stories.

*Coach Mack McCarthy*

# Dijon Pork Chops

*Dijon mustard has flavor that really sets it apart from other spices. Adding Dijon to a few simple ingredients makes a fantastic pork chop, but don't stop there. You can also apply this to tenderloins, roasts and more.*

4 pork loin chops, cut ½-inch thick
3 tablespoons Dijon-style mustard
2 tablespoons Italian dressing
¼ teaspoon pepper
¼ teaspoon thyme
Dash of cumin powder
1 medium onion, halved and sliced

In a bowl combine mustard, Italian dressing, pepper, thyme, and cumin; chill. Brown your pork chops on both sides in a skillet. Add onion to skillet. Cook and stir over medium heat for 3 minutes. Place chops and onion on a medium-high heat grill with wood chunks of your choice. Spread mustard mixture over chops and onion, and cook until juice runs clear.

# Honey-Apple Butter Pork Chops

*Jamie loves cooking chops marinated in apple butter. And honey is great for flavor. A bit of honey added to any marinade will produce a very sweet and rich taste. Top with apple butter and we are talking pork chop fantasies!*

4 (1-inch-thick) pork chops
1½ cups apple butter
¼ cup soy sauce
¼ cup lemon juice
2 tablespoons honey
½ teaspoon garlic powder
¼ teaspoon pepper

Place chops in a shallow glass dish. Combine remaining ingredients and mix well. Pour marinade mixture over chops. Cover tightly and refrigerate for several hours (overnight, if possible). Remove pork chops from marinade. Place on grill approximately six inches above medium-hot coals. Grill 10 to 15 minutes, turning and basting with marinade.

# Wine Cooler Pork

*Remember the wine cooler craze of the 1980s? This recipe is one of the first pork recipes I came up with during the college days with my first smoker.*

**1 pound boneless pork chops, cut into ¾-inch cubes**
**4 tablespoons Dijon-style mustard**
**4 tablespoons brown sugar**
**1 bottle citrus wine cooler**
**2 tablespoons soy sauce**

In self-sealing plastic bag, combine all ingredients and mix well; seal bag and refrigerate overnight, 4 to 24 hours. Remove pork from marinade, discarding any remaining marinade, and thread onto skewers. Smoke, grill or cook in the oven.

# Beer Chops

*Yep, another recipe that includes a cold beer.*

**6 bone-in or boneless pork chops**
**½ cup soy sauce**
**½ cup brown sugar**
**2 cans beer, divided**
**Salt and pepper**

Combine 1 can of beer, soy sauce and brown sugar. Marinate the chops for about two hours in the fridge. Place your chops on a hot grill using high direct heat. Turn and cook until done. Sprinkle with salt and pepper and serve. Oh yeah, drink the other beer while the chops cook.

## SMOKE NOTE

Way back in the old days, around 1937, pork was filled with loads of fat. Pork lard was an ingredient in many consumer products as well as used for cooking lard. Today the pork industry produces a much leaner pork product. According to the National Pork Board, today's commercial pig has about 73% less fat and about 50% fewer calories than its 1937 cousin.

# Honey Garlic Barbecue Spareribs

*This recipe is from a reader of my food columns who swears there is no better way than honey and garlic to flavor some great ribs. So I tried it and loved it. You can cook on a grill, on the smoker, or in an oven.*

**3 to 4 pounds pork spareribs**
**¼ cup plus 2 tablespoons**
**  honey, divided**
**1 teaspoon salt**

**2 tablespoons soy sauce**
**1 teaspoon black pepper**
**3–4 garlic cloves, crushed**
**Hot sauce to your taste**

Mix soy sauce, 2 tablespoons honey, salt, pepper, and garlic to make a marinade; marinate the ribs for 1 to 2 hours. Combine ¼ cup honey and hot sauce to your taste and brush it on the pork. Cook until done; baste with any remaining marinade for the last 30 minutes of the cooking process. Serve hot with a cold beverage, some slaw, a corn muffin and a big old brownie.

# Pork Ribs and Apple Dressing

*This recipe came from one of the many great cooks at a Civil War re-enactment.*

**2 sections spareribs**
**2 cups vinegar-based marinade**
**3 medium apples**
**2 slices salt pork**
**2 cups bread crumbs**
**¼ cup fresh parsley**

**½ cup chopped celery**
**¼ cup chopped onion**
**¼ cup sugar**
**¼ teaspoon salt**
**¼ teaspoon pepper**

Marinate the ribs in the marinade of your choice for at least 2 hours. Dice apples. Fry salt pork. Mix remaining ingredients except for salt and pepper, and spread as a paste across the arch side of the ribs. Place the second section of ribs on top and tie together with wire or cooking string, then rub with salt and pepper. Cook in covered grill or over open fire with spit.

# Backyard Grilled Spareribs

*These ribs are great with Texas toast and a big helping of beans.*

2 slabs pork spareribs
2 cups favorite marinade
1 cup ketchup
¼ cup Worcestershire sauce
1½ cups cherry cola

¼ cup vinegar
2 teaspoons paprika
2 teaspoons chili powder
1 medium onion, chopped
1 teaspoon black pepper

Marinate ribs in your favorite marinade. Prepare a medium-hot banked fire in covered grill or smoker. Cut each slab of ribs into about four sections. Place rib-side-down over indirect heat and grill for 2 hours. Meanwhile in a saucepan, combine remaining ingredients and simmer for about 20 minutes. Brush, baste and turn often.

# Parrot Head Steve's Margarita Pork

*I met Steve in Asheville when I headed there to eat some barbecue. We talked about food and Jimmy Buffet. Steve is a card-carrying Parrot Head and this is a dish he makes for summer parties.*

1 pound pork, cut into 1-inch
  cubes
1 cup margarita drink mix
  (liquid type)
1 teaspoon cumin powder
1 clove garlic, minced
2 tablespoons butter

2 teaspoons lime juice
1 teaspoon sugar
1 tablespoon parsley
2 ears corn, cut into 8 small
  pieces
1 red bell pepper, diced
1 green bell pepper, diced

Combine margarita mix, cumin, and garlic. Place pork cubes in heavy plastic bag; pour marinade over to cover. Marinate for at least 30 minutes. Blend together well the butter, lime juice, sugar and parsley; set aside. Thread pork cubes, corn and peppers onto skewers. Grill over hot coals, basting with butter mix. Rotate often and serve hot.

# Pork on a Stick

**1 pound boneless pork loin**
**½ cup red wine vinegar**
**2 tablespoons olive oil**

**1 tablespoon soy sauce**
**1 clove garlic, minced**
**¼ teaspoon oregano**

Slice your pork into thin strips and arrange in a shallow baking dish. For marinade, combine vinegar, olive oil, soy sauce, garlic and oregano; pour over the pork strips. Cover and refrigerate as long as possible, turning pork occasionally. Remove the pork strips from the marinade and save the marinade. Thread pork on skewers. Put your marinade into a small saucepan, add a little water and bring to a boil. Place skewers on grill over high heat and grill for 12 to 15 minutes. You need to turn and baste with the marinade often.

## Deck Chef Tip!

### Slice 'Em and Dice 'Em

If your recipe calls for thin cut meat strips, ask your butcher to slice it. Or place the meat in the freezer to make it harder but not rock solid. Then cut into strips of desired thickness.

# Sticky Fingers

**420 Broad Street • Chattanooga, Tennessee 37402**
**(423) 265-7427**

**2031 Hamilton Place Blvd. • Chattanooga, Tennessee 47421**
**(423) 899-7427**

Sticky Fingers is a hometown Chattanooga favorite. The restaurant was started by a small group of barbecue lovers who were high school buddies. They now offer two Chattanooga locations and others in a few other cities. The menu at Sticky Fingers has been featured in several magazines including *Southern Living*. It has great platters, plates, lunch specials and more. Sticky Fingers does not offer you small paper napkins for your "sticky fingers," they give you huge hand towels for those drips of sauce.

According to my friend Billy, the reason they hand out towels is pretty easy to figure out, "They know your gonna make a mess get-

*Nope, this is not the restaurant. The catering crew set up for a downtown Chattanooga event, The Chattanooga Market. Great art, fruits, veggies, music and Sticky Fingers Barbecue!*

ting the meat off them bones. Paper towels just aren't going to do it!" Billy was right! I had my hands full eating a plate of ribs. It's nice to see a local restaurant hit the big time with its new locations across the South. The good news is that Sticky Fingers manages to keep its small town charm at every location.

Sticky Fingers has a full menu that appeals to parents, kids, barbecue lovers and people who just want a great dinner. You can get anywhere downtown by foot from the downtown location, and their second Chattanooga location is on the loop around Chattanooga's largest mall just off Interstate 75.

Great ribs and great value can be on their lunch specials. Sticky Fingers also has a large online business where they can ship barbecue, sauces and gifts across the country.

# Grilled Ginger Pork Cube Kabobs

*Kabobs are great things. People have been cooking meat stuck on sticks for a very long time. These pork kabobs are easy and full of flavor.*

4 large pork steaks
Dashes of black pepper, crushed
  red pepper and salt
¼ cup cooking oil

¼ cup soy sauce
1 tablespoon ground ginger
1 tablespoon brown sugar

Dash each pork steak with black pepper, crushed red pepper and salt. Dice your pork into 1-inch cubes. Combine all ingredients and place everything into a large bowl or zip-top bag. Place the bag full of stuff in the fridge for a while. I like to leave it overnight. If possible turn the bag to make sure all meat is coated. Coat all of the pieces well and place onto skewers. Cook over high heat, turning often until done. You can add veggies and such if you want. Cook on a smoker, grill or even in the oven, and serve over rice.

# Tennessee Teriyaki BBQ Pork

*Make some of this Teriyaki pork with apples, add some fresh French rolls and a heaping amount of slaw and maybe some cheese, and you have a Barbecue Pork Sandwich from a nice Tennessee Volunteer football fan.*

8 boneless pork fillets
1 tablespoon salt
1 tablespoon pepper
1 teaspoon garlic
1 tablespoon hot sauce
½ teaspoon crushed red
  pepper

1 apple, chopped
1 cup barbecue sauce
  (your favorite)
½ cup olive oil
½ cup teriyaki sauce
¼ cup Worcestershire Sauce

Place your pork fillets in a glass baking dish. Season the pork with salt, pepper, garlic, hot sauce, and crushed red pepper. Cover with chopped apple. In a large bowl mix the barbecue sauce, olive oil, teriyaki sauce and Worcestershire Sauce. Cover with cling wrap. Marinate as long as possible. My Vols buddy cooks this over high heat using wood chunks, and serves it up really hot on French rolls with just about any topping you can name. And, of course, a bit of Tennessee's own Gentleman Jack whiskey.

# Oriental Pork Foil Pack

1 tablespoon vegetable oil
1 pound diced or sliced pork
1 (8-ounce) can sliced water
   chestnuts
1 cup diced bell pepper
½ cup sliced onion
2 tablespoons cornstarch
2 tablespoons soy sauce
1 tablespoon white vinegar

1 (8-ounce) can pineapple
   chunks with juice
¼ teaspoon ground ginger
¼ teaspoon salt
1 package frozen pea pods,
   thawed
1 teaspoon Cajun seasoning
   or allspice
½ teaspoon black pepper

Heat oil in skillet. Add pork and brown. Remove pork and set aside.
Add water chestnuts, pepper and onion to skillet and cook until vegetables are soft. Add cornstarch, soy sauce and vinegar and stir to
dissolve cornstarch. Add pineapple with juice, ginger and salt.
Combine pork, pea pods, and cooked vegetables with sauce in a foil
pouch. Season with Cajun seasoning and black pepper. Seal pouch
and place over medium heat and allow to steam.

# Tailgate Sliced Pork with Grilled Veggies

1 pound pork (your choice of
   cut), sliced
Olive oil
Salt and Pepper
1 yellow squash, sliced
1 green pepper, sliced

1 onion, sliced
¼ cup melted butter
¼ cup spiced rum
1 tablespoon soy sauce
1 teaspoon allspice

Brown sliced pork in a skillet with some olive oil and salt and pepper.
Combine cooked pork with remaining ingredients and wrap in equal
portions in several foil wraps. Place directly on the grill to cook the
veggies.

# Smoked Coca-Cola Ham

*Not only does Jeff Shope of Sweetwater, Tennessee, swear by this easy recipe, but he also works for Coca-Cola. I tried this recipe on my smoker with a small picnic ham. It was darned good with the apple wood smoked flavor.*

**1 half ham with bone**                **1 (2-liter) bottle of cola**

Score ham in X pattern all over about ¼-inch deep.  Place ham in an aluminum pan and pour half of the cola onto ham.  Cover and place in fridge overnight or as long as possible.  Turn and baste with cola.  Place on smoker or covered grill and cook with medium heat (about 250°).  Baste often and cook until meat thermometer reads 190°.

**Many people have sat down to a plate of barbecue and an ice cold Coke.**  Coca-Cola® dates back to around 1886.  According to the Coca-Cola Company, Styth Pemberton, an Atlanta pharmacist, developed the original formula as a medicine.  Yes, it contained very, very, very small particles of extracted coca leaves.  Another Atlanta pharmacist bought the formula for about $2,300.  When he sold the company in 1919 it was worth around $25 million.

Although many people consider Atlanta as the home of Coca-Cola, it was first bottled by Joseph A. Biedenharn at his candy store in Vicksburg, Mississippi, and the first bottling plant was actually in Chattanooga, Tennessee.

# Barry's Barbecue Place

### 85 County Road 70 • Fyffe, Alabama 35971
### (256) 623-2102

Just as you leave the foothills of the mountains in north Alabama, you run into Fyffe, Alabama. During several stops along the barbecue trail in Roll Tide Country, people asked if I was going to stop at Barry's Barbecue Place. So, of course, I had to!

Barry and Barbara Owens started their barbecue restaurant as a carry-out only establishment around 1993. Since then it has grown into a full-sized restaurant and catering business. "We have customers across the South! I even have a few around your home in Chattanooga," Barry told me. "In fact, we produce a bunch of our smoked barbecue for other restaurants. That is how good it is!"

*Barry serves homemade ice cream that is prepared in a unique ice cream maker made from John Deere tractor parts.*

But why stop there? Barry's Barbecue Place serves up some of the best homemade ice cream you could possibly put in your mouth. "I know you said you were full, but try this!" Barry said, as he slid a bowl in front of me. Two bowls later, I was hooked!

I asked Barry what he was most proud of in his establishment. It's not a favorite dish, a sauce or rub, or even the ice cream that makes him proud. "We average a 97 or 98 on our health department scores. This restaurant is clean!" he said.

**GREAT EATS:** Barry's offers several barbecue items including beef, pork, chicken and even catfish and broasted chicken. But if you are looking for a great way to top a meal, try some cobbler and a huge scoop, or two, of homemade ice cream.

# Grilled Breakfast Ham

4 to 6 slices bone-in breakfast
   ham slices
2 tablespoons brown sugar
1 tablespoon paprika

1 teaspoon cumin
½ teaspoon cinnamon
¼ cup lemon juice
2 tablespoons orange juice

Heat up your grill. (I use a sheet of foil on the grill grates when cooking this.) Mix all ingredients, except the ham. Place ham on the grill and cook for a few minutes on each side. Quickly baste ham with sauce mix. Continue to cook until sauce starts to brown. Don't over cook or the sauce may become bitter. Serve hot as a breakfast or brunch item.

# Grilled Pineapple SPAM Burgers

*I was at a trade show in Chattanooga and met Pete—a guy wearing a blue shirt with a bright yellow SPAM logo on it. Of course we started talking and he told me he got it at a SPAM cook-off in Texas. "A SPAM COOK-OFF!" I love it! Here is his recipe for Grilled Pineapple SPAM Burgers.*

1 (12-ounce) can SPAM
1 tablespoon soy sauce
Sliced green pepper
Sliced onion

¼ cup mustard
1 teaspoon minced garlic
1 (8-ounce) can pineapple slices
Sliced Swiss cheese

Slice your SPAM luncheon meat into ¼-inch slices or a bit thicker if desired. Place flat in a glass baking dish and top with remaining ingredients except cheese. Make sure to use the pineapple juice as well. Let sit as long as possible, then move slices and veggies to the grill. Cook, baste with juice, top with grilled veggies and cheese, and serve on a hamburger bun.

# Ground Pork Burgers

| | |
|---|---|
| 1 pound ground pork | ¼ teaspoon celery powder |
| ¼ teaspoon salt | ¼ teaspoon oregano |
| ¼ teaspoon pepper | Large dash garlic powder |
| ¼ teaspoon red wine vinegar | Olive oil |

Mix together ground pork and all of the seasonings, shape into 4 burgers. Brush outside of each burger with a small amount of olive oil. Grill the burgers on the grill. Serve hot with all of the normal burger toppings.

# Tailgate Beer Brats

*Head to any college or professional football game with a tailgate section and enjoy this time-honored recipe.*

| | |
|---|---|
| 1 pack bratwurst | 1 green pepper, sliced |
| 1 onion, sliced | 1 can beer (or two) |

Place your brats in a grill-safe saucepan. Cover with sliced onions and peppers. Pour a whole beer or two into the pan and boil until the veggies get soft. Serve on hot dog buns or French rolls topped with the onions and peppers.

# Chicken and Other Birds

**One of the easiest meats to grill is chicken.** And yet one of the hardest meats to barbecue is also chicken. The texture of chicken, the way the tissue is held together, the amount of fat in a chicken compared to beef and pork, and the size of a chicken all make it perfect for high-heat grilling or medium-heat indirect grilling. Low and slow barbecue methods may render your chicken pretty dry unless you are careful.

At just about any tailgate party, cook out, or barbecue, you will find great chicken dishes being served up. In this section, I have offered a few traditional recipes, some easy recipes and some other fun stuff. Grab some chicken and fire up the smoker and the grill! Oh, yeah, there's a few turkey and duck recipes here, too.

# How to Barbecue a Whole Chicken

*Here is an easy way to have the best of both worlds by using your smoker or covered grill with medium-high heat and wood chips.*

First, get a whole chicken.  Clean it out, remove any extra fat or bundles of skin, then wash and rinse it with cold water.  Next, place the whole chicken in a large pot filled with enough cold water to submerge the chicken.  Add ¼ cup salt, 1 cup apple juice, and 1 tablespoon vinegar.  Place the chicken in the water (brine) and set in the fridge for about 4 hours or overnight if possible.  Remove the chicken from the brine, and rub with some lemon juice, garlic powder, black pepper, and your favorite seasoning.  Stuff the cavity with some lemon or orange slices, garlic and chopped onion.  Use some cooking string and tie the legs together.  Or if you like big words . . . truss your chicken!

Set up your smoker or grill for indirect medium-high heat, about 250 to 300 degrees.  Use soaked wood chips for smoke.  If possible use a drip pan with a mixture of water and apple juice.  Place chicken in the smoker/grill and baste with some beer every once in a while.  You can also sprinkle with allspice, lemon pepper, Cajun seasoning, or whatever you like.  Look for an internal temp of 175 to 180 degrees.  An easy way to tell if your chicken is done is to wiggle the drumstick.  If it turns freely, then your chicken should be done.

Remember, chicken can dry out pretty quick, so make sure to baste often.

## Smoking and Grilling Chicken

- Chicken tends to dry out. Whenever you can, use a drip pan filled with water and a bit of citrus juice to add moisture to your smoke and heat.

- Heavy rubs with lots of salt tend to dry out chicken. Use rubs with less salt or don't rub the chicken the night before.

- You can keep chicken tender and moist by using a low-salt brine. Cover your chicken with cold water, add a few table-spoons of salt and a few tablespoons of apple juice. Place this in the fridge overnight. The chicken will puff up with moisture and stay real tender during the cooking process.

- If you just can't seem to smoke chicken real good, then just grill it! Chicken is perfect over 300-degree heat, grilled to perfection and topped with seasoning and sauce, and served on a bun or over a bed of rice.

- Safe chicken is good chicken. Always thaw your chicken in the fridge. It's a good idea to rinse any poultry with cold water after removing from the packaging. Make sure to wash your hands, clean your counters and utensils before moving onto another food.

- Never (ever!) use chicken that has been thawed at room temperature . . . no matter who tells you it is OK. Thaw chicken in the fridge and use as soon as possible.

# Easy Beer Can Chicken

*I have had beer can chicken at tailgate parties in many states, and all of the recipes are so simple. This one offers a bit of citrus flavor with some garlic. And, of course, beer. People are amazed about beer can chicken because they expect it to taste like old beer. . . but it is full of flavor.*

**1 (4-pound) whole chicken**           **1 (12-ounce) can beer**
**1 tablespoon lemon juice**           **1 teaspoon garlic powder**
**2 tablespoons allspice, divided**

Thaw chicken in the fridge and remove the giblets. Make sure to rinse the chicken well inside and out and pat dry. Rub the outside of the chicken with lemon juice. Sprinkle with 1 tablespoon allspice and put the remaining allspice inside the chicken. Open your beer and pour half of it into a glass. Poke a few extra holes in the top of the can. Three should do it. Pour the garlic powder into the beer can. Put the can into the chicken and use it and the legs to balance the chicken on your grill. I also use a small foil pan even on the grill. (I like to cook using indirect grilling.) Cook until skin is deep brown and internal temp is 180° in the thigh. Remove the can before serving and enjoy. Oh yeah, while the bird is cooking, you can drink the other half of the beer.

**EASY BEER CAN CHICKEN WITH A TWIST**

So you don't like beer. Well, here is an easy fix. Instead of beer, try a Citrus soda. Maybe a soda can filled with your favorite wine or wine cooler. I had a beer can chicken once with ginger ale and oranges. Heck, half the fun about a beer can chicken is knowing you used a beer can in the bird.

# Kent's Famous Root Beer Chicken

*Anne Braley, Food Editor of* The Chattanooga Times – News Free Press, *wrote a great article about my family and I appearing on the "Emeril Live" television show. The article contained several recipes from this book including the recipe that Emeril and I cooked together, and pictures of my family doing what we love to do . . . cook. The article also contained a picture of Jamie and me by the grill, and mentioned in the caption ". . . as Kent grills his famous Root Beer Chicken." Well, let me tell you how many times our phone rang from people wanting to know about Root Beer Chicken. People called for weeks wanting to know what it was and how to make it. I spent many nights emailing food lovers this simple recipe. I actually got an email back from one nice lady who accused me of leaving out a secret ingredient because it seemed too easy.*

**6 to 8 chicken leg quarters**
**1 (2-liter) bottle of your**
**   favorite root beer**
**5 cloves garlic, minced**

**1 small onion, chopped**
**Dash Salt and pepper**
**1 tablespoon brown sugar**

Place the chicken quarters in a pan or bowl large enough to hold them. Pour root beer over chicken. I usually use about ¾ of the bottle. Add garlic and onion and cover with cling wrap. Place the whole thing in the fridge overnight and place on the smoker the next day (reserve the marinade). You can also use a grill with high, direct heat. As you are smoking the chicken, pour the root beer marinade in a saucepan. Add a dash of salt and pepper and add 1 tablespoon brown sugar. Boil it down for about 30 minutes and use as a baste on the chicken.

# Oscar's BBQ

## 118 Sweetens Cove Road • South Pittsburg, Tennessee 37380
## (423) 837-0781

Oscar's BBQ sits just off Interstate 75 as you head to South Pittsburg, Tennessee. According to Oscar Ellis, the place is named after him, but his wife Sandra is the one who kept the smoke going the first 10 years or so. "We started the business when Sandra's job moved to Mexico. She has been here the whole time. I've been here every day for about two years," Oscar said.

That kind of hands-on attention has really paid off for the couple. The menu has mouth-watering pork—chopped or pulled. "I try not to make my barbecue with too much of a smoky flavor, just enough for taste. I want it moist and tasty—not dried out." Moist it is, with a smooth, yet mild, smoked flavor.

Inside the small building you will find a few tables, cool air conditioning and Oscar or Sandra greeting you with a smile from their sliding glass order window.

**GREAT EATS:** While the barbecue is very good, be sure to try some of the mustard coleslaw and even the loaded barbecue potato. If you like barbecue sauce with a kick, ask for Oscar's Hot BBQ sauce. "It's got a bit of heat to it," Oscar says. "It's not a secret . . . I just don't give it out."

**NEAT THING:** Oscar's is a great place to grab some 'que and hit the interstate again. Oscar and Sandra believe in large portions, fresh ingredients and a smile!

# Barbecue Herb Chicken

*This is one of those recipe-creations of mine that does not sound all that great until you taste it. The upside is that it is easy AND tastes great.*

6 to 8 leg quarters, thawed
1¼ cups mayonnaise
3 tablespoons honey
_ teaspoon onion powder
½ teaspoon sage
½ teaspoon tarragon

½ teaspoon thyme
½ teaspoon minced garlic
1 tablespoon parsley
1 tablespoon apple cider
   vinegar
1 can beer

Combine all of the ingredients except chicken and beer. Add chicken and marinate in the fridge as long as possible. Cook with high heat on the grill, turning and basting with the beer. If using a smoker, add ½ of the beer to your water pan and baste with the remaining brew. If needed, you can drink a beer as well. When the chicken is done, try a dash of Cajun seasoning or allspice.

# Lamar's Cajun Chicken

*Toby and Lamar Bertrand of Landry Pepper Company love good food. With seven generations of pepper farming under their belts, they really know how to spice up some food. Here is a recipe that features their own hot sauces—Cajun Gourmet Sauces. Cajun Gourmet is by far the best of all of the sauce I have ever used. Except for mine, of course.*

8 to 10 chicken leg quarters
½ bottle Cajun Gourmet
   Red Hot Sauce
½ bottle Cajun Gourmet
   Honey Mustard

1 bottle Cajun Gourmet
   Barbecue Sauce

Wash and clean chicken; pat dry. Season generously with Cajun Gourmet Red Hot Sauce and Cajun Gourmet Honey Mustard. Let chicken set overnight in a zip-lock bag. Bake or grill until done and serve with Cajun Gourmet Barbecue Sauce.

**Note:** To find out more about Cajun Gourmet sauces, visit Toby and Lamar's website at www.cajunhotsauces.com.

# Smoky Mountain Chicken Thighs

*If you ever head to the Smoky Mountains, make sure you stop by the Wonderland Hotel. Our family has been staying there for over 25 years. During a visit to the area, I was given the basics for this recipe. I added the yogurt to the brine mixture for a bit of added flavor.*

**10 chicken thighs (or more)**     **1 tablespoon salt**
**½ cup yogurt**                    **½ cup allspice**
**2 cups water**

Place the chicken in a large flat glass dish.  Mix the yogurt, water and salt together and pour over chicken.  Cover with cling wrap.  Place in the fridge overnight.  Remove from water and gently press allspice into chicken. Cover well.  Cook on your smoker.  The chicken should remain tender since it sat in the yogurt and water brine overnight.  If needed, baste gently with a beer and water mixture.

# Easy Shredded Barbecue Chicken

*You don't have to be a rocket scientist to make some good shredded barbecue chicken. I love to pick up those huge family packs of chicken (leg quarters, breasts, thighs or even drumsticks), marinate them, smoke them, coat them with a nice sauce, and then shred the meat with a fork. I serve it hot on a bun topped with slaw and sauce.*

**2 pounds chicken (any kind;**     **Allspice**
  **I buy what's on sale)**         **Salt and Pepper**
**1 cup water**                     **1 cup barbecue sauce**
**1 can diced pineapple**             **(your favorite)**
**½ cup Italian dressing**

Combine everything except the cup of barbecue sauce.  Marinate for at least two hours or more.  Set up your smoker with some good smoke, use a water pan, place the chicken in the smoker, close the lid and let it go.  Cook to an internal temp of 170°.  Remove from the smoker and quickly shred with a fork.  Pour your cup of barbecue sauce over the chicken, mix well and place the shredded chicken in a foil pan.  Place it back on the smoker for about 30 minutes to get some more flavor.

# South of the Border Grilled Chicken

*This recipe is dedicated to those people who have little or no time for recipes or cooking. Simply mix everything together and toss it on the smoker or grill. You can use drumsticks, thighs, breasts, leg quarters or even a whole chicken.*

| | |
|---|---|
| **A bunch of chicken** | **1 tablespoon vegetable oil** |
| **1 package taco seasoning mix** | **1 teaspoon garlic salt** |
| **1 can tomato paste** | **2 tablespoons lemon juice** |
| **½ cup water** | **½ teaspoon lemon zest** |

Combine all ingredients, except chicken, mixing well. Add chicken pieces; cover and marinate as long as possible. Remove chicken from marinade and grill. Pour the remaining marinade in a saucepan and boil. Baste with marinade and serve hot.

# Jamie's Grilled Citrus Chicken

*Jamie loves fruit. If she can get me to add it to a recipe she will.*

| | |
|---|---|
| **2 large chicken breasts** | **1 slice lemon** |
| **½ cup orange juice** | **1 slice onion, diced** |
| **½ cup orange marmalade** | **2 pinches garlic powder** |
| **¼ cup olive oil** | **2 pinches parsley flakes** |

Marinate chicken in orange juice and marmalade for about an hour. Don't over-marinate with this because the citrus juice may begin to overpower the meat. Cook on grill over high heat; cook until done; remove. Cook remaining ingredients on medium-high in a nonstick skillet. Add chicken and, for added flavor, brown for about 30 to 60 seconds each side. This dish is great served over pasta or rice and topped with parsley flakes. A great side dish would be a veggie melody straight from the freezer section with some added seasoning. In a pinch we have mixed all of the ingredients except the olive oil in a glass dish and cooked in a preheated 350° oven for about 45 minutes.

# Rocket Boy Hot Grilled Chicken

*I mentioned not having to be a rocket scientist in order to make great chicken. Well, this recipe is dedicated to Linda and Sonny (otherwise known as Homer). They have meant a bunch to my son and our family over the last several years. In the food business they say a way to show appreciation is to name a dish after the person. This recipe is dedicated to Linda, Homer and ALL of the Rocket Boys.*

6 chicken breasts
1 can green chilies with juice
¼ cup jalapeño peppers
½ cup diced onion
¼ cup minced carrot
¼ cup minced celery

¼ cup minced green pepper
1 tablespoon olive oil
Allspice
Salt and Pepper
1 can sliced pineapple

Combine everything except the pineapple slices. Marinate for at least two hours or more in a zip-close bag. Place your chicken on the grill, and baste often with remaining sauce. Cook to an internal temp of 170°. Towards the end of the cooking process top, the chicken with the pineapple slices.

This chicken is great served with steamed veggies, rice or even over fresh cut greens.

# Grilled Chicken on a Stick

*Use a skewer for this chicken-on-a-stick recipe. You can use tenders, breasts, wings or whatever.*

1 package chicken tenders
½ cup yogurt, any flavor
½ cup orange juice
¼ cup steak sauce

¼ cup diced green onion
2 tablespoons minced garlic
1 pack sweet and low
1 teaspoon cayenne pepper

Marinate chicken in yogurt for about two hours. Combine orange juice, steak sauce, and all other ingredients in a small dish. Coat chicken before piercing chicken with skewers. Cook chicken on grill or in oven until done. Baste a few times with extra sauce to keep tender.

# Grilled Ginger Almond Crusted Chicken

*This chicken is great served over rice or sliced up and served hot on a couple of pieces of grilled Texas toast. A perfect dinner for two.*

1 egg, beaten
1 tablespoon milk
¼ cup flour
Salt and pepper
2 large chicken breasts

¾ cup sliced almonds
1 tablespoon butter
1 teaspoon ginger or
  1 teaspoon brown sugar
Lemon slice

Mix egg and milk; beat. Mix flour, salt and pepper. Dip chicken in egg and milk mixture and then roll in flour. Repeat. Take almonds and press into chicken until covered. Place on some foil or a disposable baking sheet and cook in a covered grill using high heat (400°) for about 20 minutes with soaked wood chips. Cook until chicken is firm and almonds are golden. Mix butter and ginger. Melt in microwave and then pour over chicken. Squeeze a drip or two of lemon as well for a bit of added flavor.


# Grilled Atlanta Jerk Chicken

*This recipe comes from the chef at a hotel in Atlanta where my wife and I stayed the night before she went in the hospital to have our son. After talking with the nice lady chef for a bit, she told my wife and me that her favorite foods were the ones she grilled at the house. She whipped up a batch of her homemade jerk chicken for us to try.*

2 chicken breasts, cut into 4
  strips each (or 8 large
  chicken tenders)
½ cup vinegar
½ cup pineapple juice
  (or orange juice)

1 tablespoon crushed red
  pepper
1 tablespoon brown sugar
1 tablespoon allspice
4 rings onion, chopped

Mix vinegar and juice; add chicken and soak for about 10 minutes (she actually put the chicken in a zip-lock bag with the juice mix, and rolled it and pressed in between her fingers). Next, skewer the chicken and grill for about 10 minutes, turning often. Remove from heat and spread dry ingredients on a dish. Roll the chicken in the mix and return to grill for a few more minutes. Serve hot.

# Spencer B's BBQ

## 6581 Highway 41 • Ringgold, Georgia 30736
## (706) 935-7675

**P**ull up, jump out and walk to the window at Spencer B's—great BBQ is only a few minutes away.  Spencer B's BBQ is owned by Chuck and Cindy Armstrong who believe in serving great 'que.

Jeff Oxford gave me a rundown of what makes Spencer B's a great place. "We only slow cook our meats. Nothing is rushed.  We season our pork with a secret blend, and the chicken and beef is flavored by slow cooking with hickory smoke."

My brother-in-law and Spencer B's employee, Jeremy Holder, cooked a perfect pulled beef plate topped with sweet barbecue sauce and a huge side of Cajun fries and some great coleslaw.  While I was licking my plate clean, Jeremy appeared around the corner and offered a quick tour of the smoker. "Watch your eyes!" Jeremy said.  "We are finishing up some ribs, so I can open this up for you to see."  Jeremy put on some thick oven gloves and lifted the massive lid of the 1000-pound smoker, and a cloud of hickory smoke boiled out.  "We build the small fire on this side and keep the ribs over here.  That way they are slow cooked and fall off the bone."

**GREAT EATS:**  Pork, beef, chicken and more.  According to the staff, one local favorite is the loaded potato.  "It's covered and smothered with everything!"  Don't miss out on their coleslaw.  "We have people come up and buy the slaw by the gallons," Beth said. Kids will be happy as well because of the large kids' menu that has everything from tenders to dogs to hamburgers and more.

**NEAT THING:**  Two picnic tables (or the hood or tailgate of your vehicle) make for great outdoor dining on a cool evening.

# Easy Smoked Italian Dressing Chicken

*This is an easy way to make chicken for the smoker, grill or even oven. While I prefer the smoker, the grill does wonderful as well. This recipe is a time saver.*

6 chicken breasts
1 bottle robust or zesty
  Italian dressing

1 cup fresh shredded Parmesan
  cheese (use canned cheese,
  if needed)

The trick to this is to put the chicken in a freezer bag, pour in the dressing and leave it in the fridge for a day. If you don't have time, then an hour or so will still taste pretty darned good. Place the chicken in the smoker, on the grill or in the oven, and cook until done. If you are using a smoker, try a milder wood such as a fruit wood. I have had success with apple and pear wood. If using a grill, cook over high heat and baste often. If cooking in the oven, you may want to quickly brown the outside edges in a skillet, place the chicken and the dressing in a glass dish, cover with foil, and bake at 350° for about 45 minutes. However you cook this dish, when it is done, place it on a platter and top with cheese.

# Rolled Chicken & Cheese

*This simple recipe is an awesome bite-sized finger food that can also be a great main dish to any dinner menu.*

4 to 6 chicken breasts
8 to 12 slices Swiss cheese
1 small onion, sliced

1 green pepper, sliced
Allspice

Place chicken breasts on wax paper and cover with another sheet of wax paper. Pound to ½-inch thick or less. Layer the remaining ingredients on the chicken and roll up. Secure with a toothpick and wrap in foil. Place the foil packs on the grill over medium heat. Serve hot with rice or veggies.

# Sassy Loraine Chicken

*My buddy Robin Loraine Neal loves her daughter, her husband, her family, and because she is Italian, she loves great food. "I'm Italian—it's in my blood!" So when Robin tells me to call Jeff for a great steak recipe, get in touch with Chef Michael for a few fresh ideas or write down one of her recipes, I listen. Here is Robin's recipe for her "sassy" chicken.*

**4 boneless, skinless chicken breasts**
**½ cup chopped onion**
**½ cup chopped bell pepper**
**2 tablespoons minced garlic**

**1 small hot pepper**
**1 cup honey**
**Sliced Pineapple**
**¼ cup sesame seeds**

In a small skillet, mix onions, bell peppers, garlic, and hot pepper; brown on medium heat for about 5 minutes. Cover and let cool. In a large glass casserole dish, mix honey and pepper/onion mixture. Add chicken breast, baste, cover and refrigerate. You have now created a sweet and spicy glaze for the chicken to marinate in overnight. When you are ready to cook the chicken, top with pineapple slices.

**JAKE SAYS —**

Turning chicken with tongs instead of a fork prevents the juices from running out and keeps the chicken moist and flavorful.

You can either grill or bake the chicken in the oven at 350° covered for 45 minutes. If you chose the oven, allow the chicken to remain in the marinade while baking. If you grill, be sure to glaze the chicken every few minutes with the sweet spicy perfection. . . a little Italian, with a little spicy pepper sass! Top with sesame seeds and serve.

# The Easiest Grilled Chicken Wings in the World

20 to 30 chicken wings and mini drumsticks
1 bottle your favorite barbecue sauce
3 tablespoons honey
2 tablespoons hot sauce
1 tablespoon minced garlic
Salt and pepper to taste

Place everything in a big bowl and coat the chicken evenly. Grill over high heat. Turn often and baste with any remaining sauce. Serve hot with your favorite dressing on the side.

# Smoked Chicken Parmesan

*Yes, you can make a great Chicken Parmesan on the smoker or grill. Just prepare the recipe below in a cast iron skillet or other grill-safe skillet, and toss it in a smoke-filled chamber for the final cooking session.*

4 boneless, skinless chicken breasts
½ cup milk
1 egg, beaten
1 cup Italian Seasoned Bread Crumbs
⅓ cup olive oil
10 slices mozzarella cheese
1 cup spaghetti sauce
1 teaspoon garlic powder
½ cup Parmesan cheese

Clean and dry your chicken. Dip chicken breasts in a combination of milk and egg, then in bread crumbs. Brown in olive oil on both sides until golden. Arrange on the skillet evenly and top with slices of cheese. Pour sauce over cheese, sprinkle with garlic powder and Parmesan cheese. Place the whole skillet in a covered smoker or covered grill with lots of hickory smoke, and cook for about 30 minutes to an hour to fuse in the flavor and until the chicken is done. You can add more layers of cheese if needed. Cheese really soaks up wood flavor.

# Smoked Chicken Salad

*This recipe comes from my sister-in-law, Tonya. Bless her heart, Tonya married my brother Scot, who, like me, believes any organized sport deserves a good cookout. Tonya is a professional in the chef and catering world. I took her original recipe and added flavor by using smoked chicken breasts. You can always make it with boiled or baked and cubed chicken, but why waste all that great flavor?*

**4 hickory smoked chicken
  breasts, cubed
1 medium onion, diced
4 stalks celery, diced
¼ cup Dijon mustard**

**⅔ cup mayonnaise
1 tablespoon basil
1 tablespoon garlic
1 tablespoon black pepper
⅓ cup sliced almonds**

Mix all ingredients together and place in a covered bowl for a few hours before serving to let the flavors get going.

# Jim's Leftover Barbecue Chicken Salad

*I met a guy named Jim during a trip to Virginia who swears by this chicken salad recipe. He says he made this recipe, which offers a great combination of flavors, when he had some leftover barbecue chicken and wanted something different. Use any barbecue chicken and break it into small pieces; I used leftover leg quarters.*

**1 pound leftover barbecue
  chicken
1 can mixed vegetables,
  drained
1 can whole kernel corn,
  drained**

**½ cup chopped scallions
½ cup mayonnaise
1 tablespoon mustard
Salt and pepper to taste**

Mix everything together and let rest for a few hours in the fridge before serving on bread.

# Cajun Deep-Fried Turkey

*Chances are if you have been around the Southern Appalachian Mountains for any length of time, then you have tried, heard of, or had a friend give you a fried turkey.*

1 (10- to 15-pound) wild turkey
5 gallons peanut oil
1 cup brown sugar
½ cup hot sauce

5 tablespoons Cajun seasoning
2 sticks butter or margarine
1 teaspoon each: garlic powder
and cayenne pepper, if desired

Thaw turkey in fridge and pat dry excess water. Tie NON-MELTING STRING such as cotton to the bird so that you can lift him in and out of fryer. Pour peanut oil into a 10-gallon pot. Put pot on propane cooker and heat oil to 375°. Add sugar and hot sauce. Carefully submerge turkey in oil. Deep fry for 3½ to 4½ minutes per pound; continue to cook until turkey floats to the top. Remove bird from oil; immediately dust heavily with Cajun seasoning. Melt butter; add garlic powder and cayenne, if desired. Brush turkey with butter mixture. Allow to cool for about 15 minutes before carving.

**CAUTION:** PLEASE ONLY USE FRYERS OUTDOORS AND UNCOVERED.

## Deck Chef Tip!

### Quick Measure

Here is an easy way to determine the exact amount of oil needed to fry a turkey. Heed my advice here lest you have cooking oil spilling over the sides of your cooker into the open flame. (I don't have to tell you how bad that would be.) Before frying your turkey, fill the fryer completely with water. Drop the bird into the fryer allowing the excess water to spill over the sides. Remove water until it covers the bird by about an inch. Remove the turkey and measure the water that remains in the fryer. That is precisely how much oil you will need for deep frying your turkey.

# Buddy's Bar-B-Q

**5806 Kingston • Knoxville, Tennessee 37919**
**(865) 588-0051**

I make several trips a year between north Georgia and Lexington, Kentucky, via Interstate 75. Along the way, I often find myself at one of the Buddy's Bar-B-Q locations. Even though Buddy has passed away, the family-owned business still follows his community-minded lead with involvement in fund raisers for cancer research, senior citizens homes, schools, churches and even a scholarship fund.

Buddy's is a small, regional chain of restaurants that feel like a down-home, family-owned barbecue joint, even the ones attached to gas stations along the interstate.

Buddy, who was in the loan business at the time, and his wife Lamuriel came to the Knoxville area in 1954. They were disappointed they could not find any local barbecue to suit their tastes. In 1967, Lamuriel bought a small drive-in restaurant in Seymour. Soon Buddy was out of the loan business and helping his wife at the restaurant. They added barbecue to the menu and saw an increase in sales of more than 240%.

They have been in business for over 30 years and have 12 company-owned stores, three franchised stores, and a full-scale catering department.

**GREAT EATS:** Call me a sucker for good, simple sides, but the hush puppies served with Buddy's meals are awesome.

# Smoked Lemon Turkey

*Smoked turkey dates back as long as people have been eating turkey. The recipe is very simple and uses traditional spices and flavors. It makes a fantastic main dish.*

**1 (14- to 16- pound) turkey**
**½ cup lemon juice**
**½ cup extra virgin olive oil**
**½ tablespoon thyme**
**½ tablespoon ginger**

**½ tablespoon rosemary**
**½ teaspoon crushed black pepper**
**Very small dash of garlic powder**

Take about 3 cups of mesquite or hickory chips and soak in water for about an hour. When you cook a larger bird such as a turkey, you need to use a water pan circled by hot coals and wood chips. Get your coals all fired up and spread them in a circle around pan filled with water and some citrus juice of your choice. The trick to using wood chips and chunks is to bring the chips to smoke by placing them on hot coals, and when smoke appears, move to a cooler spot in the grill before adding your meat.

It would be great to rub your turkey down with a mixture of all of the ingredients the night before you cook, but if time does not permit then just do it while your charcoal is getting ready. Rub the turkey down with some olive oil and lemon then spread spice mixture over the bird. Place turkey breast-side-up on the center of the grill directly above the pan of water and juice. Place a meat thermometer in the turkey without touching a bone. Cook your bird to an internal temp of 175°. It could take up to 6 hours depending on the size of your bird and the temperature of the coals.

# Barbecue Turkey

1 (14- to 16-pound) turkey
1 cup vinegar
1 cup brown sugar
½ cup olive oil

½ teaspoon garlic
½ teaspoon ginger
½ teaspoon pepper

This recipe is similar to the lemon turkey recipe, except that you need to marinate the turkey in vinegar and brown sugar while it thaws. Make sure you thaw it in the fridge. Brush with remaining ingredients before cooking.

The trick to great smoked and barbecue turkey is keeping the smoke going, so keep some extra soaked wood chips on hand. Also, keep the lid closed as much as possible. But if you have to open the lid, then also make sure you baste. If you notice that some edges are burning, then lightly cover them with some foil.

# The Ultimate Turkey Burger

*After many attempts, most turkey burgers are really bland. But I think I have come up with a very nice ground turkey burger.*

1½ pounds fresh ground
   turkey
1 loose cup fine chopped ham
½ cup minced green pepper
½ cup fine chopped scallion
½ cup shredded jack cheese
½ cup crushed cracker crumbs

¼ cup minced onion
¼ cup soy sauce
1 heaping tablespoon minced
   garlic
1 teaspoon salt
1 teaspoon pepper
½ cup olive oil

Combine all of the ingredients except for the olive oil. Press into 4 to 5 burger patties. In a skillet pour in the olive oil and quickly brown each side of your turkey burgers. Remove from the olive oil and place on a covered grill with hickory wood chips and finish cooking. These are perfect served on an onion roll with some Swiss or provolone cheese melted on top. I made a quick sauce from sour cream, hot sauce, taco sauce, garlic and cumin powder to use instead of traditional mayo.

# Deck Chef Tip!

## Leftover Turkey

Got some leftover turkey from the holidays or the last time you deep fried a bird? Well here are a few ideas for leftover turkey.

### Turkey Enchiladas

Take some leftover turkey, grated cheese of your choice, diced onion, pepper and tomato, and warm in a small nonstick skillet. When heated, dash with a bit of cumin powder and Cajun seasoning, and roll in a flour or corn tortilla. Serve hot.

### Quick Turkey Chili

Open a can of your favorite chili, or make some from scratch. Dice some leftover turkey and toss it in. Serve over corn chips and top with cheese and/or chopped onions. Quick and delicious.

### Turkey Philly

Slice some leftover turkey, and warm in a sauce pan with a bit of steak sauce or Worcestershire sauce. Add sliced onions and bell peppers. Place on a French roll and top with your favorite cheese.

# Grilled Duck Made Easy

*Chicken and turkey rule the grill on weekends, but every once in a while you may want to try something different. Here is an easy recipe for grilled duck from a hunter buddy of mine.*

**1 whole duck**
**¼ cup olive oil**
**2 lemons**
**¼ cup butter**

**1 tablespoon salt**
**1 tablespoon pepper**
**1 tablespoon thyme**

Rinse duck with cold water and pat dry. Rub with olive oil. Chop lemons into quarters and squirt some juice on the duck. Dash on some (not all) salt, pepper and thyme. Stuff with remaining lemons, salt, pepper and thyme. Cook on the grill over medium high heat. You may need to top with a bit of foil to prevent burning. Turn and baste often with wine. You can also use the oven at about 400° for 45 minutes or so. Nick says that duck is great served with any citrus fruit.

*Reminders of years gone by are hidden under brush and in many nooks and valleys in the Appalachian Mountains.*

# Roasted Pepper Orange Duck

*This recipe is a combination of spicy and fruit flavors. You can use any variety of duck, large, small, whole, breasts or whatever. The secret is in the seasoning.*

| | |
|---|---|
| 1 whole duck | 3 tablespoons hot sauce |
| Salt and pepper | 2 tablespoons grape jelly |
| 4 small oranges | 1 teaspoon thyme |
| 1 small lemon | Dash parsley |
| 4 tablespoons Worcestershire | Dash of paprika |
|   sauce, divided | ½ cup white wine |

Wash and rinse your duck in cold water and pat dry. Sprinkle with salt and pepper inside and out. Slice oranges and lemon into thin strips and squirt some juice over the duck. In a bowl, mix 2 tablespoons Worcestershire sauce with hot sauce, jelly, thyme, parsley and paprika. Stuff the duck with the oranges and lemon. (If you are not using a whole duck then just add the fruit to the marinade.) Place the duck into a glass baking dish and pour over the liquid mixture; cover with cling wrap and place in the fridge. Marinate the duck in the sauce for about an hour or so. Be careful not to over-marinate, or the flavor of the meat may be overpowered. Cook in a preheated 350° oven. Depending on your choice of duck, the cooking time could be anywhere from 40 minutes to an hour or more. Baste with wine to keep the duck from drying out.

# Jordan's Bar-B-Q

**910 Stuart Road • Cleveland, Tennessee 37312**
**(423) 478-2171**

When you turn off I-75 at Cleveland, Tennessee, heading east towards the mountains, you will pass Jordan's BAR-B-Q on Paul Huff Parkway. Dennis Jordan worked for years helping many people run their restaurants better. "I worked for a food wholesaler. My job was to help people buy the right products, help them determine costs and things."

After years of helping others, Jordan and his wife decided to open their own restaurant. "Barbecue was an easy decision. I knew barbecue, and that was about all the size of our building would allow us to make." In fact, the size of the building determined the whole menu. "We did not have room for fryers or any of that stuff, so our menu started small. Barbecue, chips and a cold drink with a few other sides." Today the restaurant has grown several times and the menu offers just about everything.

Take a walk around back and check out the custom-designed smokers. "This one was so heavy, we had to have a big crane lift it off the truck. I designed it and had a company build it." Mr. Jordan said.

**GREAT EATS:** MASSIVE pulled pork plate or the stuffed Bar-B-Q potato.

**NEAT THING:** Ride the piggy out front.

# Wild Game

**Don't get me wrong, pork is king in the South,** but when settlers moved into the Appalachian Mountains, the woods were filled with available meats for hunting and cooking. Some of the wild game that was available, according to the National Park Service, included wild pig or boar, catfish, deer, squirrel, trout, chicken, rabbit, turkey, and more.

This may sound all well and good, but somebody had to go out and hunt 'em, kill 'em, clean 'em, and then cook 'em. That was a lot harder back in that day than it is now. And remember this, these days if you go hunting all weekend and don't get anything, you can still stop by the burger hut and get a big burger meal with a cola and an order of super-sized fries.

I must admit that I'm not the biggest hunter in the world (but I do like to fish). That means I was kinda short on the whole wild game cooking area. What better way to get some really great recipes than to talk to hunters? Wether you hunt, know someone who hunts, or simply want to apply these recipes to meat you can pick up at the grocery store, I know you'll enjoy their recipes.

# John's Smoky Mountain Wild Boar Ribs

*When John Pauza of Cleveland, Tennessee, is not knee deep in the advertising world, he is hunting. John is a hunter that has great recipes for just about anything he hunts. This is John's recipe for some great wild boar. As John says, "First you have to get a boar!"*

**2 racks wild boar ribs**
**1 tablespoon crushed red pepper**
**1 tablespoon black pepper**
**2 tablespoons salt**
**4 cups barbecue sauce (your favorite)**

Remove excess fat from the ribs and place in covered roasting pan. Rub spices into meat, cover, and slow cook in an oven at about 200° for 2 to 3 hours. Remove from oven and baste with sauce, then cook on a covered grill or smoker with hickory for about 2 more hours, using medium indirect heat. Baste before serving. John likes to serve this with some steak fries and cornbread.

# Barbecued Wild Boar

**1 (5-pound) wild boar roast**
**2 quarts water**
**1 cup beer**
**3 beef bouillon cubes**
**2 cans chicken broth**
**1 teaspoon garlic powder**
**1 bottle your favorite barbecue sauce**

Preheat over to 300°. Place meat in a roasting pan with all the ingredients except barbecue sauce. Cook 4 hours, basting often. Remove roast and strain liquid, saving 1 cup. Return roast to pan and top with barbecue sauce. Pour 1 cup of strained liquid around roast in pan. Reduce oven temperature to 250° and cook for 1 hour.

# Barbecue Deer Roast

*I'm told by my hunting buddies that the older a deer, the longer the meat will need to marinate.*

| | |
|---|---|
| **1 (4-pound) venison roast** | **1 tablespoon minced garlic** |
| **½ cup vinegar** | **1 cup water** |
| **¼ cup brown sugar** | **½ cup ketchup** |
| **1 stick butter, melted** | **¼ cup mustard** |
| **1 tablespoon salt** | **1 large dash crushed red pepper** |

Place the roast in a foil pan. Combine remaining ingredients and pour over roast. Smoke, using hickory with high indirect heat. Baste often with sauce.

## Deck Chef Tip!

### Walk on the Wild Side

Before buying or cooking any wild game, check with your local Agriculture Extension office for any tips they may have on wild game cooking for species in your area. Also check with the Extension office for any health warnings that may have been issued. I have found that just about every office is loaded with info on safety, cooking tips and often recipes.

# John Pauza

## Hunter and Wild Game Cook

**T**he great thing about my buddy John Pauza is that he always has a great story. He once told me about the time a buddy of his brought a live squirrel into the local Waffle House. The guy met John and his late friend Donnie to drop off the squirrel because he knew John had a squirrel cage. He had the squirrel wrapped in a towel and tucked inside a bag. Of course the little critter escaped and ran all over the place before being cornered.

When NOT chasing squirrels around Waffle House, John likes to hunt and cook. It seems to me that he has hunted just about anything you can eat, and he has a recipe for any game you name. Here is his very simple recipe for Buttered Squirrel. "This does not taste like chicken," John says.

# John's Buttered Squirrel

**3 or 4 cleaned squirrels, diced**
**2 cloves minced garlic**
**2 tablespoons butter**

**½ cup flour**
**Salt and pepper to taste**

Soak squirrel in iced salt water overnight. (A salt water soak is called a brine.) Rinse, dredge in flour, garlic, salt and pepper and pan fry in some butter until browned. Serve hot!

# Broiled Lemon Squirrel

*This recipe comes from a Civil War buff and a big time hunter buddy of mine. It's very simple.*

**2 squirrels, dressed fully**
**Salt and pepper to taste**
**1 lemon**

**1 stick butter**
**Breadcrumbs**

Dress two fat squirrels, split them open on the back, rinse them very clean in cold water, season them with salt, pepper and the grated peel of the lemon; broil them on a gridiron over clear coals, turning and basting them two or three times with butter. When they are well done, place them in a warm dish, sprinkle on a handful of grated bread, and pour on two ounces of drawn butter.

# Country-Fried Beaver Steaks

*Terry from North Carolina tells me that beaver tastes like venison. According to Terry, trapped beaver was a staple in the "old days." I'm not sure if he was around in the old days, but he seemed to know what he was talking about. So here is a recipe for beaver steaks.*

**2 beaver steaks, about**
  **½-inch thick**
**2 cups self-rising flour**
**1 tablespoon minced garlic**
**1 teaspoon salt**

**1 teaspoon pepper**
**2 medium onions, chopped**
**1 cup bacon grease or lard**
**1 can cream of chicken soup**
**1 can sliced mushrooms**

Soak beaver in water overnight. Combine flour, garlic, salt and pepper in a zip-close bag; add the steaks and shake until coated. Place the onions in a skillet and add lard or bacon grease; heat. Fry the beaver steaks. Add chicken soup and mushrooms; simmer and serve hot.

# Barbecued Rattlesnake Chunks

*I'm told rattlesnake is quite good grilled, baked or fried.*

**1 large rattlesnake, cut into
  chunks about 2 inches thick**
**2 cups barbecue sauce**

**1 tablespoon of hot sauce**
**1 teaspoon whiskey**

Combine all of the ingredients in a covered dish and marinate in the fridge, overnight if possible. Place the entire contents into a foil pan and lightly cover with foil. Cook in a covered grill with high heat for about 45 minutes. Snake meat dries out easily, so turn often to keep the meat coated, and keep lightly covered with foil while cooking.

# Barbecued Armadillo

*I can't say I've tried this recipe. I don't even know where you get armadillo meat! But I'm told this is good and that I should give it a try.*

**2 pounds armadillo meat**
**1 stick butter, melted**
**1 tablespoon lemon juice**
**1 teaspoon onion salt**

**1 large dash salt**
**1 large dash pepper**
**1 cup barbecue sauce
  (your favorite)**

Brush the armadillo meat with the melted butter and lemon juice. Rub the armadillo meat with the onion salt, salt and pepper. Wrap in foil and cook in a covered grill with high heat for about 45 minutes. Remove foil; add more butter if desired and allow to brown. Before you serve, baste with barbecue sauce. Cook to heat up the sauce, and serve hot.

# Roasted Ale Rabbit

*Word-of-mouth recipe from a Civil War re-enactor.*

**1 rabbit, fully dressed**
**Salt and pepper, to taste**
**¼ cup vinegar**

**1 spoon sorghum syrup**
**1 cup beer**

Rub rabbit with salt and pepper; soak in vinegar, sorghum and beer for a good while. Cook over open flames by tying rabbit to a stick and holding it over the fire. Baste and turn often. Rub again with salt and pepper and eat.

## JAKE SAYS —

Wild game may need to be brined. This helps remove any extra blood or fluids. A seasoned brine will also help marinate tougher, leaner cuts.

# Burra Burra BBQ & Steakhouse

**5075 Highway 64 • Ducktown, Tennessee 37317**
**(423) 496-2001**

Just past the beautiful mountain waters flowing through the rapids of Ocoee River sits Ducktown, Tennessee. This neat little town is home to The Burra Burra Company—World Class Barbecue. After years of working in the white water guide business, Ben and Sharon Griffith decided to open a business based on one of their passions—barbecue.

The name Burra Burra comes from the local mine that operated in Ducktown from 1850 until 1958. "The mine was so big it could be seen from space," Sharon said. The mine produced high-grade copper ore and was named after a rich copper mine in Australia.

Ben showed me his smoker that opens into the back of the kitchen. As he swung open the massive doors, he told me the story about finding it. "These college guys down South decided to open a barbecue stand and couldn't even cook. They closed up and I came in a bought it from them. I know this is the best barbecue this smoker has ever produced."

**GREAT EATS:** Burra Burra serves up a great plate of pork, beef and chicken. Menu items also include burgers, salads, sides, and a kids' menu. Don't overlook the Brunswick Stew! It is AWESOME!

**NEAT THING:** Check out the old pictures and photos from the mine and town hanging on the walls. The history of the area is amazing to look at. Also, the cooler and scales in Burra Burra are throwbacks in time and add a great touch to the restaurant.

In memory of Ben who left us too early.

# Catfish, Crawfish and More!

**Most of us think of catfish or trout** when the subject of "seafood" comes up in the South or the Appalachian region. After traveling around eating at many barbecue restaurants, I discovered that many menus offer a rather diversified seafood fare. Sure, some menus offer popcorn shrimp to kids. But many also offered seafood dishes that are not only traditional, but down right high class!

I know that not many streams in the mountains have shrimp, grouper or lobster in them. Many Smoky Mountain culinary experts, however, have discovered that with today's quick shipping, fresh seafood is available. With that in mind, here is a rather broad sampling of recipes, dishes, tips and tricks for cooking your "catch of the day" (even if you catch it at the local grocery store).

# Up In Smoke Bar-B-Cue

## 804 McMinnville Highway (Highway 70)
## Woodbury, Tennessee 37190 • (615) 563-5046

For nearly all his life David "Porky" Scott drove a truck across the highways and byways of the South. "I drove a bunch of miles," Scott said. "I ate a lot of barbecue, too!" Somewhere along the way, Scott, or Porky to his friends, learned the great art of barbecue. Today Porky has his own restaurant just five minutes east of Woodbury, Tennessee. "I've had folk from the Carolinas, Texas, and Memphis come through here, and they all like what they ate!" Porky said. "In fact some grand champion once told me that he was glad I didn't do contests, because then he would have lost a spot!"

Up In Smoke Bar-B-Cue is in a small building just off the road. The design of the building is great. The garage-type kitchen is accessed by a small window from the inside prep area. "I need a rack of ribs!" Crystal Hodgson yells through the window for a customer. In a few seconds some hot, juicy ribs were passed through. The smoker building is about the same size as the restaurant. "The smoker is custom made. It has three pits and a deep fryer with three tanks of gas and plenty of space for wood. When I cater, I open the garage doors and tow the whole thing out!" Smoker and trailer weighs over 6,000 pounds.

Up In Smoke Bar-B-Cue serves up some very nice pulled pork. The sauce is AWESOME!

**GREAT EATS:** My son says the tater wedges are great. I had a pulled pork sandwich topped with sauce and slaw . . . very nice.

**NEAT THING:** The neatest thing on the menu, however, is the smoked barbecue bologna. Try it!

# Grilled Catfish Fillets

*This is a healthier version of a great Southern catfish recipe. No batter, no breading and it's not fried. But it's still full of flavor!*

6 catfish fillets
½ cup melted butter
3 lemons, juiced
1 tablespoon lemon zest
1 tablespoon hot sauce
1 teaspoon mustard

2 tablespoons Worcestershire
  sauce
1 teaspoon salt
1 teaspoon pepper
1 teaspoon paprika

Combine all ingredients, except catfish, and let rest. Rub a dash of salt and pepper on each fillet and place the catfish on oiled grill grates. Baste the fillets frequently as you cook. Cook evenly over medium-high direct heat.

# Spicy Grilled Catfish

1 teaspoon lemon-pepper
  seasoning
1 teaspoon white pepper
1 teaspoon Creole seasoning
1 teaspoon blackened fish
  seasoning

2 tablespoons lemon juice
4 catfish fillets (1⅓ pounds)
Vegetable cooking spray
Lemon wedges and celery
  tops for garnish

Combine first 4 ingredients in a small bowl. Sprinkle lemon juice and seasoning mixture on both sides of fish. Spray a wire fish-basket with cooking spray; place fish in basket. Grill fish, covered, over medium coals (400°) for 7 to 10 minutes on each side, or until fish flakes easily when tested with a fork. Remove fish from basket, place on a serving platter, and garnish with lemon wedges and celery tops.

# My Favorite Recipe for Fish Brine

1 quart water
½ cup non-iodized salt
½ cup sugar
3 ounces rum
1 ounce lemon juice

3 garlic cloves, pressed
3 tablespoons pickling spice
¼ teaspoon lemon pepper
3 bay leaves

Mix all ingredients until dry ingredients are completely dissolved. Add fish to brine and refrigerate 8 to 12 hours. Remove fish from brine and pat dry to remove any excess water before using in your recipe. Excess water (brine) can ruin a great seafood batter or corn meal breading. You also don't want to be around a bunch of hot oil when you toss in a piece of fish dripping with brine.

# Jimmy's Hot Fish

*This recipe will make some spicy catfish. You can even add more hot sauce to bring it up another level or two. If you don't like catfish, pick a few fillets of your favorite fish and start cooking! Submitted by Jim W.*

8 to 10 catfish fillets
2 cups of water
2 tablespoons hot sauce
2 cups self-rising yellow
   cornmeal
1 cup all-purpose flour
2 teaspoons salt

1 teaspoon minced garlic
1 teaspoon black pepper
1 teaspoon garlic powder
1 teaspoon paprika
1 teaspoon chili powder
Vegetable oil

Place the catfish fillets in a glass baking dish and cover with a mixture of water and hot sauce. Cover with cling wrap and keep in the refrigerator for about two hours, then drain. Combine cornmeal and remaining ingredients, except for the oil, in a plastic bag. Place the fillets one at a time in the bag and gently roll to coat evenly. Don't shake too hard or the fillet may break.

Heat the oil to 375° and fry fillets about 4 minutes on each side or until golden brown. Drain well on paper towels. Serve hot.

# Deck Chef Tip!

## How to Brine Fish

Brines are talked about a few times in this book, but while a fish brine it still just a brine, it can be a bit different. A brine is a simple, saltwater mixture used to soak meats. It adds moisture and flavor and removes oils, etc. The difference between brining fish and brining other meats is the amount of time you leave the meat in the brine solution. Fish is often a very delicate meat and over-brining can damage it or make it taste pretty bad.

Brining fish is really simple. Just place fish in the solution. You want to make sure the meat is covered, so you may need to place a weight, such as a small bowl or coffee cup, over the meat to hold it down into the brine mixture. Next, place your bowl with the brine and submerged meat in the refrigerator.

So how long do you brine? It depends on how thick the meat is and what type of meat you are using. Thinner, more tender cuts require less time, such as five hours or so. Thick chunks of meat may need to be brined for 12 hours. Remove fish from brine and lightly rinse each piece under cold water. Lay on a paper towel for several minutes.

## Simple Fish Brine

½ cup non-iodized salt          1 quart water
½ cup sugar

Stir until everything is completely dissolved.

# Country-Fried Catfish

*Get the deep fryer going or cook them up in a skillet. However you do it, here is an easy recipe for traditional country-fried catfish.*

**2 pounds catfish, cleaned and skinned**
**½ cup flour**
**Salt and pepper to taste**

**½ cup yellow cornmeal**
**Pinch granulated sugar**
**Shortening, bacon fat, or oil for frying**

Dry fish with cloth or paper towel. Combine dry ingredients. Dip fish into the cornmeal mixture and fry in hot shortening until golden brown on each side.

## JAKE SAYS —

Different types of seafood require different temperatures for cooking.

## GRILLING TIP

In general, fish fillets and seafood steaks tend to cook the best over a medium-hot heat source. On the flip side, shellfish require a high heat source for proper cooking.

# Grilled Bass Fillets

*If you have ever been fishing in the South, then you know what a bass is. Nothing beats the feeling of a bass taking a lure with a massive jolt on your line. Try this simple recipe for great bass.*

**3 pounds bass**
**2 tablespoons butter**

**Salt and Pepper to taste**
**1 teaspoon oregano**

Wash the bass and pat it dry. Spread butter over each fillet and place on grill. Sprinkle with salt, pepper, and oregano while you cook. Do not overcook bass. Turn as few times as possible.

# Hillbilly Blackened Sea Bass

*Who says a country boy can't cook some sea bass? That's the great thing about interstate highways. Every time I hit the coast with the family, we try some new recipes when we get home. Here is a very simple way to blacken a nice cut of sea bass.*

**4 to 6 sea bass fillets**
**2 tablespoons melted butter**
**1 teaspoon olive oil**
**2 teaspoons paprika**
**1 teaspoon minced garlic**

**1 teaspoon thyme**
**½ teaspoon black pepper**
**½ teaspoon cayenne pepper**
**½ teaspoon lemon zest**

Rinse your fillets, pat dry and set aside. Melt the butter and stir in olive oil. Combine all of the remaining ingredients in a small bowl. Gently brush the butter and olive oil over the fish. Sprinkle about half the seasoning mix over the fillets. Grill over high heat. On your last turn, use the rest of the dry mix with a bit of the butter and oil, and gently coat the presentation side of bass. I finish this dish in the oven for about 3 minutes under a hot broiler. Serve hot with a few slices of lemon or lime.

# Mud Creek Restaurant

**804 County Road 213 (Old Highway 72)**
**Hollywood, Alabama 35752 • (256) 259-2493**

Around 1947, people in the Hollywood, Alabama, area rented small boats and marina space from Lex Carver. The arena sat on Mud Creek off Highway 72. During the summer the marina was packed, but during the fall and winter, business dropped way off. In order to

keep some cash flow coming in, Lex decided to open a small barbecue restaurant during the cooler months. Soon the barbecue was as popular as the fishing! "Cars used to line up the highway to grab a take-out of barbecue," Gerry Teal, son-in-law of Lex said.

"When the restaurant first opened, it sat on the marina, had a few stools and a table or two. The main part of the business was walk-up." Today, the brand new dining area holds about 200 people. Where else can you walk into a barbecue restaurant with walls covered in fishing photos and a great view of the water where fishermen bring in their catch?"

Mud Creek offers great barbecue pork, huge pieces of catfish, fresh veggies and more. According to Gerry, the barbecue is the main fare, the catfish comes second, and people really seem to enjoy the sauce!

**NEAT THING:** Check out the pictures of Lex and his pals from years past holding huge stringers of fresh-caught fish. On a quiet day you can just about hear the laughter from hundreds of summer picnic goers from years gone by enjoying the warm days on Mud Creek.

# Apple Marinated Tuna Steaks

*This is a quick marinated fish recipe that uses the natural flavor of apples.*

3 cups apple juice
1 cup brown sugar
1 cup soy sauce
1 teaspoon salt
1 teaspoon of garlic salt

1 teaspoon of onion salt
½ teaspoon lemon pepper
½ teaspoon black pepper
4 tuna steaks

Combine all ingredients and pour over the tuna steak and let marinate overnight, if possible. Grill over medium high heat. Boil remaining marinade and use as a baste.


# Smoked Fish Chunks

*This recipe is from a guy I met in Florida. He processes fish. He started saving small and broken pieces, then tried cooking them in different ways. The easy way was battered and fried, but his favorite is this recipe for Smoked Fish Chunks.*

2 pounds your favorite fish,
  brined
1 cup yogurt

¼ cup buttermilk
Salt and pepper to taste

Marinate brined fish in yogurt and buttermilk for about two hours. Place fish in a foil pan with marinade. Put the pan into your smoker. I usually use fruit woods with fish, but of course hickory is perfect. Depending on the thickness of your chunks, smoke time could be from 4 to 7 hours. If you grill the fish with wood chips for smoke, grill over medium-high heat until the fish is easy to flake with a fork.

# Orange-Marinated Gulf Fish

*We don't know what happened to Tubby, but he could make some great fish. He made an Orange-Marinated White Fish that I ate like crazy. When I went back to Florida to get the recipe, Tubby was gone. So I made one up. Enjoy!*

1 cup orange juice
Zest from orange
¼ cup white wine
¼ cup olive oil
2 tablespoons Cajun seasoning

1 tablespoon minced garlic
1 tablespoon Dijon mustard
Salt and pepper to taste
6 to 10 white fish fillets

Combine all of the ingredients, except the fish, and mix well. Marinate the fish for about an hour or two in the fridge. Grill over high heat. Boil the remaining marinade and use as a baste. Serve hot with tartar sauce spiced up with a bit of orange juice and a dash of pepper.

# Plank-Smoked Fish Fillets

*Here is a great recipe to start your cedar-plank-smoked-fish-fillet cooking career. Fish fillets with some skin left on will hold up better to cedar-plank cooking, but try different types of fish and fillets to find the one that works best for you.*

2 large fish fillets of your choice
2 tablespoons olive oil
1 tablespoon black pepper
1 teaspoon cayenne pepper

½ teaspoon salt
½ teaspoon thyme
½ teaspoon allspice

Center fish on the soaked cedar planks, skin side down. Brush with oil; sprinkle with black pepper, cayenne pepper, salt, thyme and allspice. Gently rub the seasoning into the fish. Place your plank over the heat source. Cook on medium heat until fish flakes, about 15 to 20 minutes. Serve hot with a squeeze of lemon juice.

# Deck Chef Tip!

## Using a Cedar Plank

Cedar planks can be a great tool when grilling fish. The wood keeps the fish moist while the aroma of the wood gives the fish incredible flavor. Be sure to buy a quality plank. You can buy cedar planks from any decent outdoor grilling shop. They can also be ordered online from several sources. Don't use planks that are treated or processed. These can contain chemicals and other material that will make your fish taste bad, and can also make you sick!

About a half hour before grilling, place the plank in cool water. You may need to place a plate or other heavy object over the plank to help keep it under water. Soak the plank for about 30 minutes, turning it after 15 minutes so that the side covered by the plate can get an even soak as well.

Cedar-plank grilling works best over charcoal or wood chunks that have a light cover of ash. With gas grills, the wood will dry out and catch fire. So if you use gas, make sure the heat is turned down low.

# Grilled White Fish

*White fish is a great, inexpensive fish packed with flavor. It can be cooked in fillets or broken up for other dishes. This recipe comes from a chef buddy who was originally from Mobile, Alabama.*

**2 pound white fish fillets**　　　**1 tablespoon lemon**
**¼ cup spiced rum**　　　　　　　**Salt and pepper to taste**

Place a layer of foil over your grill grate. Spray with nonstick spray before starting fire. Grill fish, basting with rum, a squirt of lemon, salt and pepper. White fish can be thin, so turn only once, if possible.


# Easy Grilled Swordfish

*Swordfish can intimidate people for some reason. I think we are all so used to pre-cut, battered fillets, that most of us have never even thought about trying other types of seafood.*

**4 (1-inch-thick) swordfish steaks**　　**1 teaspoon sugar**
**2 tablespoons butter**　　　　　　　　**1 teaspoon garlic powder**
**2 tablespoons soy sauce**　　　　　　　**Sesame seeds, optional**
**1 tablespoon hot sauce**　　　　　　　**Salt and Pepper to taste**

Wash swordfish and pat dry. Combine the remaining ingredients and spread over each steak evenly. Wrap each steak as tightly as possible in cling wrap and place in the fridge until grilling time (at least an hour). Grill over medium-high heat. Turn once and grill each side about 5 minutes. (Time may vary due to the thickness of the cut and the heat of your grill.) The steak is done when thickest part flakes with a fork.

# Deck Chef Tip!

## Grilling Seafood

- When cooking seafood on the grill, make sure your grill grates are clean, oiled and hot before placing the fish on the grill.

- A great gadget to have on hand is a seafood grilling basket which will allow you to turn the whole basket instead of trying to flip each piece of fish.

- When cooking seafood on the grill, turn it only once. Every time you turn a fillet, the weaker it gets, which could make it break.

- Always cook seafood starting with the dark (or skin) side up. Fat stored under the skin will soak back into the fillet, adding to the natural flavor.

- Citrus juice is a great seasoning for just about any type of fish fillet.

- Use a fork or butter knife to gently lift the fillet away from grill grates. Then slide your spatula under the fish fillet to turn.

- Most fish fillets change from a translucent color to an opaque color as they cook. In general, six to 12 minutes of cooking time per inch of thickness is sufficient.

- Fish, as well as almost every other meat, will continue to cook some after it is removed from the heat source.

# Crystal Springs Smokehouse

**505 West Ninth Street • Chickamauga, Georgia 30707**
**(706) 375-9269**

While you're in town visiting the National Military Park in Chickamauga, Georgia, be sure to head south of the battlefield for a great barbecue dinner. Just off the main road on West Ninth Street sits a very humble log cabin—home of Crystal Springs Smokehouse.

With the great smell of hickory all around it, Crystal Springs is very cozy, not small, just cozy. During my first visit to Crystal Springs, the customer sitting in the booth next to me and I talked about the news on the TV that was hanging in the corner. By the end of the conversation we had discussed baseball, politics, cars, football, and more. Now that's cozy.

You'll find paper towels on each table along side a bottle of Crystal Springs Smokehouse sauce which goes great on their pork sandwiches as well as their beef and chicken.

**GREAT EATS:** Crystal Springs Smokehouse offers up everything from barbecue to salads, plus burgers, and a host of sides. They also offer a kids menu and a varied assortment of family packs. My order was simple—a pork sandwich, side of slaw, and some tea. A classic barbecue meal. Delicious.

**NEAT THING:** The walls reminded me of a hunting lodge and make for a very comfy place to enjoy a meal.

# Grilled Grouper Filets

*The cook at a barbecue restaurant that has since been replaced by a highway expansion gave me this recipe a while back. They served it with their house barbecue sauce mixed with tartar sauce on the side. NICE!*

**1 pound fresh grouper**
**2 cups salsa**

**1 tablespoon lemon juice**
**1 tablespoon Cajun seasoning**

Marinate your grouper in a baking dish with the remaining ingredients. Grill until flaky and serve hot.

# Easy Fried Trout

*If you are ever around these parts, make sure you go trout fishing along the mountain streams. If you don't catch any, don't worry, just head to the local fish market, and definitely try this recipe from S. L. Canner in North Carolina.*

**2 pounds rainbow trout fillets**
  **(or whole trout)**
**1 teaspoon salt**
**1 teaspoon pepper**
**1 egg**

**1 teaspoon milk**
**1 cup self rising flour**
**¼ cup self-rising cornmeal**
**Oil for frying**

Sprinkle trout inside and out with salt and pepper. Beat egg and blend in milk. In a separate bowl, mix flour and cornmeal. Dip fish in egg/milk mixture and roll in flour/cornmeal mix. Place fish in frying pan containing ⅛ inch cooking oil. Cook on moderate heat until golden brown on both sides (approximately 10 minutes, depending on thickness of fish).

# How to Make a Foil Fish Boat

Use some heavy-duty foil and tear off pieces about 3 inches bigger, on all sides, than your fillet. Layer two pieces of foil for each fillet. Place your fillet in the center of the foil and fold the sides up to form an opened-topped boat around the fillet. Top the fillet with your favorite seasonings, a bit of butter or whatever you wish. Pinch the opened ends firmly shut, then place on a covered grill. The foil boat keeps the fish from sticking to the grill. It will also keep the seasonings and flavors from dripping away.

# Cajun-Grilled Crawfish

*After our house burned, I turned to a good buddy to help fill sauce orders. Toby and Lamar's family have been growing peppers and making hot sauce down bayou way for about seven generations. Toby swears by a good bunch of spicy crawfish like the ones below.*

12 ounces frozen, peeled and deveined shrimp
½ cup butter or margarine
4 cloves garlic, sliced
¼ cup fresh lemon juice
1 tablespoon dehydrated parsley flakes
½ teaspoon seasoned salt
½ teaspoon lemon and pepper seasoning

Cook garlic in butter for 2 to 3 minutes; add remaining ingredients, except shrimp, and heat until blended. Put shrimp in shallow dish; pour marinade over shrimp and let stand for 1 hour. Thread shrimp on metal skewers and cook 5 minutes per side. Turn and baste occasionally. This recipe makes 4 servings.

# Kent's Garlic Shrimp

*Man, shrimp is great for grilling and tailgating. Here is a great tip. Thread the shrimp on dual skewers so they will not fall through the grill grates. They will also be easy to turn.*

**12-ounce package de-veined, frozen shrimp**
**½ cup melted butter**
**1 tablespoon minced garlic**
**¼ cup lemon juice**

**¼ cup lime juice**
**1 tablespoon spiced rum**
**1 tablespoon parsley**
**½ teaspoon allspice**
**½ teaspoon Cajun seasoning**

Thaw your shrimp and combine with the remaining ingredients in a glass baking dish. Cover and let rest in the fridge for about an hour. Thread the shrimp onto skewers and grill for about 5 minutes; turn. Turn about 2 or 3 times. Serve hot.

# Hot Shrimp Boil

*We used to often visit a local restaurant that specialized in spicy crawdads and shrimp. They also had some huge sandwiches. Here is the secret recipe for a good, old-fashioned shrimp boil.*

**1½ pounds large, deveined shrimp**
**2 quarts water**
**1 cup hot sauce (less if desired)**
**2 tablespoons minced garlic**
**2 small onions, diced**
**2 lemons, sliced**

**¼ cup pickled jalapeño**
**2 tablespoons salt**
**2 teaspoons cumin powder**
**2 teaspoons mustard**
**2 teaspoons black pepper**
**1 teaspoon celery salt**

Combine all ingredients in a large pot and boil for about 20 to 30 minutes. Serve hot with a few lemon or lime wedges.

# Easy Grilled Po Boy

*This is kinda like cheating, but it's good.*

Take a bunch of frozen, battered shrimp or fish sticks and cook them in the oven, skillet or whatever. Sprinkle with Cajun seasoning while still hot. Place a handful in the center of a French roll with a bit of your favorite white cheese. Smear some butter on the French rolls and wrap in foil. Toss them on the grill to keep warm and melt the cheese. When you serve them, keep them in the foil and allow your guests to add lettuce, tomato, onion or whatever. Top with spicy tartar sauce and enjoy. This is perfect for precooking and serving hot at a tailgate party.

*After any raft outing you can always bank on some great barbecue. This is my buddy Lisa and her family. Rafting is HUGE in the mountains. Very big business and restaurants are often nearby jump-out points and rest stops along the more popular rivers.*

# Dips and Salsas

**Nothing beats a great bowl of dip** or a zesty salsa as pre-barbecue munchies.  If you don't have much time on your hands and MUST use the usual tub of bland store-bought dip, add some zest by tossing in some spices and/or crushed-up bacon.  And don't stop with the normal chips and crackers to use as dipping scoops.  Add some veggies, fruit and even breadsticks.  I've given you some really good and really EASY recipes to get you (and your next cook-out) started.

# Jones Memorial United Methodist Church

### 4131 Ringgold Road • East Ridge, Tennessee 37412
### (423) 629-9388

About 30 years ago the late Tom Martin started a small fund raiser at Jones Memorial United Methodist Church in East Ridge, Tennessee. The small barbecue dinner was held to raise money for needy people in the community. To hear church members tell it, the fund raiser was small but effective. Today the annual barbecue is HUGE and still very effective.

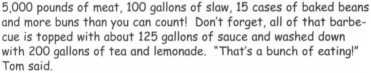

According to Chairman Tom Baugh and his son Jeff, the barbecue will serve more than 5,000 pounds of meat, 100 gallons of slaw, 15 cases of baked beans and more buns than you can count! Don't forget, all of that barbecue is topped with about 125 gallons of sauce and washed down with 200 gallons of tea and lemonade. "That's a bunch of eating!" Tom said.

The cooking starts about three days before the weekend sale. The pits are fired up, trucks arrives with meat, pork, beef and chicken. Then the smoking begins. "We still use the original sauce that they used 28 years ago. We also have a secret rub," Jeff said. When the cooking is done, the food is served by an army of volunteers. "The volunteers really make this thing go. This year we even have our Cub Scouts helping carry trays and clean tables," Tom said as he waves to a local politician eating a big sandwich.

The proceeds of the event buy coats and jackets for children in the area.

# Spicy Cream Cheese Dip

*Another easy dip. Everyone will ask how you made it.*

1 package taco seasoning
1 (8-ounce) package cream
  cheese, softened

½ cup sour cream
1 tablespoon hot sauce
1 teaspoon minced garlic

Mix all in a bowl, cover, chill and serve. For added flavor, toss in some chopped onion, garlic or minced peppers.

# Beer Cheese Dip

½ cup beer
½ teaspoon Tabasco sauce

1 pound processed cheese loaf,
  cut into 1-inch cubes

Mix all ingredients in a saucepan. Cover and cook on low until cheese melts. Stir until mixture is smooth.

# Mexican White Cheese Dip

1 cup finely shredded
  Monterey Jack cheese
1 (4.5-ounce) can chopped
  green chilies
¼ cup half-and-half

2 tablespoons minced onion
1 teaspoon ground cumin
½ teaspoon salt
1 tablespoon finely chopped
  fresh cilantro, optional

Place all the ingredients in a double boiler and cook over medium heat, stirring occasionally, until melted and well blended. Be careful not to overcook.

# Jamie's Baked Sourdough Bowl Cheese Dip

*Just when you think you can't add anything new to a cookout, party or get together, place this incredible dish on the table. Submitted by Jamie Whitaker*

1 sourdough bread bowl
2 packs softened cream cheese
4 cups shredded Cheddar
  cheese
½ cup bacon bits

½ cup chopped green onion
1 teaspoon steak sauce
Dash crushed red pepper
Dash black pepper

Take sourdough bread loaf and cut about an inch off the top. Hollow out loaf to make a bowl, leaving walls and bottom a little less than 1-inch thick. Save pieces. Combine remaining ingredients well. Spoon into bread bowl, making sure to pack it in tight. Bake in oven, uncovered, at 350° for about 20 minutes. Dice the saved bread into small pieces and use for dipping.

# Taco Dip

*Man, talk about easy. This is a great dip that is quick and simple.*

Smear about a quarter inch of cream cheese on the bottom of a small glass-baking dish. Then spoon an even layer of refried beans, then a layer of hot salsa, then maybe some black olives, chopped lettuce, some chopped peppers, then some cheese, diced tomato etc., etc. Chill and serve. You can add more toppings, peppers and spices to fit your taste. Serve chilled with chips on the side.

# Spinach Dip

*While I can't say spinach is my all-time favorite food, many people love spinach dip. So here is a quick recipe.*

1 (10-ounce) package frozen chopped spinach, thawed and drained
16 ounces sour cream
8 ounces cream cheese, softened

2 teaspoons Dijon mustard
1 envelope instant onion soup mix
½ cup chopped almonds
½ cup chopped onions
1 teaspoon minced garlic

Mix all together, cover and chill before serving.

# Easy Spinach Dip

1 cup mayonnaise
1 cup sour cream
1 envelope dry ranch dressing mix

1 (10-ounce) package frozen chopped spinach, thawed and drained

Mix ingredients and chill before serving

# Even Easier Spinach Dip

*When you are really pressed for time, here is how you make spinach dip.*

1 (10-ounce) package frozen chopped spinach, thawed and drained

1 large container ranch dip

Mix it and eat it!

# Pizza Dip

*Kids love pizza. So next time you have a big cookout and need a kids' dip, make this simple recipe and surround the dish with breadsticks, pretzels, crackers and corn chips. I tried this at a housewarming party and was hooked.*

8 ounces cream cheese,
  softened
2 tablespoons Parmesan
  cheese
1 teaspoon Italian seasoning
½ teaspoon garlic powder

1 small jar of pizza sauce
1 can mushrooms, drained
¼ cup minced pepperoni
1 cup shredded mozzarella
  cheese

Soften the cream cheese and mix with the Parmesan cheese then spread onto the bottom of a 9-inch pie plate. Sprinkle with Italian seasoning and garlic powder. Cover with pizza sauce, mushrooms and pepperoni. Top with mozzarella cheese and bake for about 15 minutes until thoroughly heated and cheese is melted.

# Honey Mustard Dip

½ cup mayonnaise
1 tablespoon mustard
1 teaspoon minced onion

¼ cup honey
1 tablespoon parsley
1 dash season salt

Mix all ingredients in a bowl and serve as a dip or salad dressing.

# Easy Honey Mustard Dip

*This could possibly be the easiest known recipe in the world (except for Even Easier Spinach Dip on page 183 which has only two ingredients).*

3 tablespoons Dijon mustard
2 tablespoons honey

A bit of garlic powder

Mix and serve.

# Onion Ring Dipping Sauce

*This is a very easy version of that great dipping sauce you get with those whole fried onions. It's great as a dip, and I have added it as a topping to sandwiches.*

⅓ cup mayonnaise
2 teaspoons ketchup
2 tablespoons cream-style
  horseradish
½ teaspoon cayenne pepper

¼ teaspoon paprika
¼ teaspoon salt
⅛ teaspoon oregano
Dash of salt and pepper
Dash of garlic powder

Mix all together and serve chilled with onion rings and such.

# Thick Brown Sugar Dipping Sauce

*Whenever we cook out, there seems to be a large number of kids running around. Since the advent of chicken nuggets, many of them expect a thicker sauce like they find at their favorite fast food restaurant. Here is a simple version that is perfect for dipping.*

1 cup ketchup
¼ cup steak sauce
⅓ cup brown sugar

1 tablespoon apple cider
  vinegar
1 teaspoon garlic

Combine all ingredients in a bowl and stir. Make sure the brown sugar is completely dissolved. Chill to thicken and serve.

# Shrimp Dip

¼ cup milk
1 cup mayonnaise
1 teaspoon hot sauce
1 tablespoon Worcestershire
  sauce

¼ teaspoon garlic salt
1 onion, diced
8 ounces Cheddar cheese
5 ounces small precooked party
  shrimp

Place in a blender and blend well. Chill and serve.

# Red Barn Barbecue

**1151 County Road 849 • Sylvania, Alabama 35988**
**(256) 638-8342**

For years Ken and Kay Johnson talked about opening a small restaurant. The idea simmered in their minds for years until Ken was locked out of his job for months. "We started during that time with the help of our kids. I went to a friend's barbecue restaurant in Kentucky, and he taught me his method," Kay said. Ten days after returning to work at the end of the lockout, Ken decided that he was in the barbecue business for good.

Even on a slow Saturday, cars continue to turn off the main road into the gravel and grass loop driveway of Red Barn Barbecue. I asked how a small place built off the main road in a field attracted business. "Word of mouth. I have never had to advertise. People know we have a quality product," Ken said as he handed a bag of barbecue sandwiches out of the window to an outstretched arm. Kay said that many customers appreciate their simple menu as well. "We do barbecue pork, chicken and ribs." Red Barn also offers some great homemade sides and a massive barbecue potato.

**GREAT EATS:** Make sure you save room for some of Kay's cobbler.

**NEAT THING:** There are lots of neat things about Red Barn Barbecue—the building, the location and more. Getting a chance to talk with Kay and Ken is a blast. Ken is also a pastor at a small church. They love what they do and advise anyone thinking about getting into the barbecue business to make sure that they are work-a-holics.

# Cajun Tuna Dip

*A bit different, but real tasty. Another spicy recipe from my good friends Toby and Lamar Bertrand at the Landry Pepper Company.*

1 stick butter
1 small onion, chopped
1 bell pepper, chopped
1 can mushroom soup

1 medium sized can white tuna, drained
Cajun Gourmet Red Hot Sauce to taste

Melt butter; add onion and bell pepper and cook until clear. Add mushroom soup and tuna. Season to taste with Cajun Gourmet Hot Sauce. Serve hot in a chafing dish with Fritos or party crackers.

**Note:** Use Cajun Gourmet Habanero Sauce if you like it really hot.

# Easy Salmon Dip

*My sister-in-law, Tonya, introduced me to salmon dip. She challenged me to eat it and guess the ingredients. I came close, but she finally relented and gave me the recipe so I'm sharing it with you. This recipe is quick, easy, and delicious.*

1 (14-ounce) can red salmon, drained
1/3 cup light cream
2 (3-ounce) packages cream cheese, softened
Large dash celery salt

1/4 cup lemon juice
1 tablespoon dill weed
1 tablespoon parsley
1 teaspoon minced onion
1/2 teaspoon minced garlic
Salt and pepper to taste

Combine all of the ingredients in a bowl and mix until smooth. Cover and refrigerate until ready to serve.

# Ultimate Barbecue Bean Dip

*This is one heck of a dip. Perfect with a big bag of dipping chips.*

½ cup browned ground beef
1 can refried beans
½ cup barbecue sauce
¼ cup sour cream
¼ cup minced onion
¼ cup minced green pepper

¼ cup minced jalapeño
   peppers
1 small can tomato paste
2 tablespoons hot sauce
1 teaspoon cumin powder
1 teaspoon minced garlic

Mix everything together in a glass baking dish and bake in a 325° oven for about 20 minutes. Top with shredded cheese, if desired.

# Easy Barbecue Dip

*I know we have all heard of dipping sauce but this is a true barbecue dip. It's great for chips, carrots or whatever you like to dip.*

½ cup fine shredded barbecue
½ cup barbecue sauce
½ cup shredded jack cheese

½ cup sour cream
¼ cup minced onion
1 teaspoon bacon bits

Combine all ingredients, cover and chill.

# So Simple Yogurt Honey Fruit Dip

**1 (8-ounce) container non-fat
  vanilla yogurt**

**¼ cup honey
2 tablespoons ground cinnamon**

Mix all ingredients together and chill before serving with sliced fruits.

# Peanut Butter Yogurt Dip

**2 tablespoons peanut butter
1½ cups of your favorite
  yogurt**

**1 tablespoon dark brown sugar**

Put the peanut butter in a bowl and add about a spoonful of yogurt to soften the peanut butter into a thinner cream. You can add more if needed. When the peanut butter is creamy and easy to blend add the rest of the ingredients and mix well. Chill and serve.

## Deck Chef Tip!

### Don't Forget the Fruit

Trying to be a bit on the healthy side? Fruit dipping trays are great. Get some sliced fruits and make an easy dip out of your favorite yogurt. You can use any flavored yogurt and simply add in a few extras. But, be careful. Sometimes added ingredients, like sugars and honey, can break down the enzymes in the yogurt so that creamy and cool fruit dip you made most likely will be drippy goo the next day. Plan on using it for the meal then toss any remaining dip.

# Creamy Caramel Dip

*What cookbook would be complete without a caramel recipe? This recipe is perfect for fall, apples and kids.*

8 ounces cream cheese,
  softened
¾ cup brown sugar
8 ounces sour cream
2 teaspoons vanilla extract

Squirt of lemon juice
1 cup cold milk
1 box instant vanilla pudding

In a mixing bowl, combine cream cheese and brown sugar. Mix until smooth. Add sour cream, vanilla, lemon juice, milk and pudding mix. Mix well, chill and serve with fresh cut fruits or cubes of pound cake on toothpicks.

# Easy Fruit Salsa

1 mango, peeled and pitted
1 cup diced strawberries
2 small oranges, peeled
1 cup raspberries
¼ teaspoon salt
1 tablespoon ginger

2 tablespoons lime juice
2 tablespoons lemon juice
1 tablespoon cider vinegar
1 tablespoon sugar
½ teaspoon crushed red pepper
½ teaspoon cumin powder

Dice the fruit into small pieces (minced if possible). Add remaining ingredients and mix well. Cover and chill before serving.

# The Chattanooga Salsa Queen

*Lysa Burns-Brown of Chattanooga, Tennessee is a hoot! Not only is she funny, friendly and pretty . . . she can also make some great Salsa. According to Lysa, she has tried just about every version of salsa made and a few more: "I've tried many variations from store-bought to authentic Mexican restaurant servings. As far as I can tell, they all use the same thing: tomatoes, onions, hot peppers. I believe 'variety is the spice of life' . . . why should salsa be any different?" So instead of buying some salsa Lysa came up with this recipe using not only a variety of flavors but a variety of color as well. She says, "It makes an attractive presentation, not that the guys would take their eyes off the football game to notice!!"*

**6 to 8 fresh tomatoes, chopped**
**1 green bell pepper, chopped**
**½ red bell pepper, chopped**
**1 orange bell pepper, chopped**
**2 small, red chili peppers,**
  **chopped**
**⅛ small habanero pepper,**
  **chopped**

**3 to 4 jalapeño peppers,**
  **chopped**
**1 sweet yellow onion, chopped**
**⅓ bunch cilantro, chopped**
**1 teaspoon salt**
**Juice of 1 lime**

Set aside ½ of the chopped tomatoes in a separate bowl. Place remaining tomatoes and the other chopped vegetables in food processor. Add cilantro. Pulsate until chopped to desired consistency. Add salt and lime juice and pulsate until well blended (5 to 7 seconds). Pour into reserved tomatoes and stir, making sure to blend together thoroughly. Chill in bowl 3 hours.

Pour into sterilized jars. Serve with chips suitable for dipping. Viva La Mexico!!

# Sweet Corn Salsa

*Here is a nice salsa recipe that has the flavor and texture of sweet corn.*

1 (16-ounce) can whole kernel
corn
1 tomato, fine diced
1 (4-ounce) can green chilies
1 jalapeño pepper, diced
¼ cup chopped green bell
pepper

¼ cup chopped green onions
2 tablespoons white wine
vinegar
1 tablespoon vegetable oil
¼ teaspoon salt

Mix all ingredients. Cover and refrigerate until chilled, about 1 hour.


# Cajun Caviar

*A former co-worker turned me on to this dish. I usually put it out as a snack before dinner is served. It can also be used as a great topping to grilled chicken.*

1 medium-size avocado, peeled,
seeded, and minced
1 large, ripe tomato, diced
1 small onion, chopped
½ cup finely chopped scallions
1 teaspoon minced garlic
2 tablespoons red wine vinegar

1 tablespoon vegetable oil
1 tablespoon hot sauce
½ teaspoon cumin powder
½ teaspoon chili powder
1 can black eye peas
1 can whole kernel corn
Salt and pepper to taste

Place all ingredients into a bowl and mix. Cover and chill before serving with big corn chips.

# Breads

**Most people that know me pretty well** know that the chances of me picking up a store-bought loaf of bread are pretty slim. On those rare occasions when I do pop into the grocery store for a loaf of bread, I always buy Sunbeam because that is what I grew up with. I think I may have even had a crush on the Sunbeam girl in their logo when I was about 8 years old. I know my son likes his plain white bread. And I, of course, use buns and rolls. But given the chance, I will hit a local bakery or the bakery section of my grocery store for some fresh bread. Nothing beats bread fresh from an oven and delivered across the counter, instead of across the country in the back of a truck. Here are a few recipes for breads from traditional loaves, to beer bread and even hush puppies. Have fun, and remember when you want some good bread, head to your local bakery. If anything, just for the aroma.

# National Cornbread Festival

South Pittsburg, Tennessee
www.nationalcornbread.com

South Pittsburg, Tennessee, is located in the shadows of rising mountains and hills and nestled along the banks of the Tennessee River. Every year the town hosts the National Cornbread Festival. The event is every April and includes a cornbread cooking contest, recipes, food vendors, arts and crafts.

The smell of cornbread cooking in Lodge cast iron skillets fills the air. As well as the aroma of the many food venders cooking up great foods. The festival also includes a large number of arts and craft vendors and even live music.

The National Cornbread Festival is a very fun event for people that love food other than

*The wait in line was over 20 minutes long for tasty samples in "Cornbread Alley" at the National cornbread Festival.*

the normal carnival foods. Historic South Pittsburg has tons of great history including the name of the county, Marion, which is named after a Revolutionary War Hero nicknamed "The Swamp Fox." Stop by the National Cornbread Festival for some really GREAT food and a fun family weekend.

# TR's Carolina Ramp Cornbread

*A ramp is a plant that grows along the foothills of the Appalachian Mountains. It is almost a cross between an onion and garlic with a spicy type of flavor. If you want to get right down to it a ramp is in the leek family. Submitted by pit master T.R., Carolina Mountains*

2½ cups cornmeal
1 cup self-rising flour
2 cups buttermilk
1 cup water
2 eggs, beaten

6 tablespoons sugar
1 tablespoon salt
½ cup chopped ramps
  (or green onion)
1 cup shortening or ⅔ cups oil

Combine all. If using shortening, melt it first. I bake mine in an outdoor brick oven off my smoker. I have also cooked it in an indoor oven at about 400° for about 30 minutes. I use a cornbread mold or a muffin pan. If needed, I add a bit more buttermilk.

# Kent's Cracklin' Cornbread

*This is a simple recipe for an old southern favorite. You will find cracklin' bread across the South in restaurants and at church pot lucks and festivals. Enjoy!*

1 pound bacon, fried crisp and
  crumbled
1 teaspoon salt
⅔ cup minced onion
1½ cups self-rising cornmeal
½ cup self-rising flour

2 eggs, beaten
¼ cup honey
¼ cup sugar
½ cup milk
1 cup orange juice

In an oven-safe (iron) skillet, cook bacon and reserve about half of the bacon fat. Combine remaining ingredients and mix into a thick batter. Heat the reserved bacon grease in a preheated 350° oven. Carefully add batter to pan and bake for about 30 minutes. You can use a traditional cornbread pan but the texture wont be the same.

# Kent's Famous Barbecue Cornbread

*The trick to making Kent's Famous Barbecue Cornbread is barbecue. I use left over barbecue, beef or pork, that has been shredded fine and re-smoked on the smoker for about an hour using hickory wood. This adds that deep barbecue flavor that you can sink your teeth into. You can "Kick Up The Sauce On Top A Notch," as Emeril said by adding a bit more hot sauce. What ever you do just remember that this cornbread slices better if given a few minutes to cool. It is great served with white beans and a side of slaw.*

## CORNBREAD:

½ pound left over barbecue pork or beef
1 cup butter, melted
¼ cup milk
1 cup sugar
4 eggs
1 (15-ounce) can cream-style corn
½ (4-ounce) can chopped green chile peppers, drained

½ cup shredded Monterey Jack cheese
½ cup shredded Cheddar cheese
1 cup all-purpose flour
1 cup yellow cornmeal
4 teaspoons baking powder
¼ teaspoon salt

Preheat oven to 325°. Lightly grease a 9x13-inch glass baking dish. Shred left over barbecue into fine pieces. In a large bowl, beat together butter, milk and sugar. Beat in eggs one at a time. Blend in cream corn, chiles, both cheeses, and barbecue. In a separate bowl, stir together flour, cornmeal, baking powder and salt. Add flour mixture to corn mixture; stir until smooth. Pour batter into prepared pan. Bake in preheated oven for 1 hour, until a toothpick inserted into center of the pan comes out clean. Or better yet, until the center is firm to the touch.

## TOPPING:

¼ cup butter
2 tablespoons your favorite barbecue sauce

1 tablespoon cayenne pepper
1 tablespoon garlic powder

Combine all and melt in microwave. Brush over cornbread and place back in oven for a few minutes. Cut into squares and serve warm – or, break into pieces and serve in a small bowl.

# BEHIND THE SCENES

**A year ago,** if you had asked me if I thought a barbecue cornbread recipe was good enough to get my family and I flown to New York City to cook with possibly the most famous chef in the country, Emeril, I would have said "No." But that is just what happened when I submitted a recipe to a contest hosted by the Food Network. Many people asked for the recipe I submitted, but due to contracts with the Food Network I could not tell anyone or give the recipe out until the day of the show. That's all part of TV magic. Anyway, here is that recipe— thought up late at night, made from left over stuff in the fridge, and sent in by a Deck Chef who was gently forced to do so by his wife!

## JAKE SAYS —

The secret to Kent's cornbread is that he puts some water and vinegar on the shredded barbecue and re-smokes it for an hour or two which really seals in the hickory flavor.

## TASTY TIP

Any cornbread recipe can be spiced up a bit by adding extra ingredients. Try everything from creamed corn, hot peppers, bacon, taco meat, a bit of cheese and even what Kent did ... barbecue.

# Sweet Buttermilk Cornbread Muffins

*Mr. Cook comes by often and one of the topics we always seem to chat about is bread. He owns a chain of specialty bakery restaurants, Panera Bread, as well a grocery store with a great deli. I asked him what he would consider to be the Southern Appalachian areas most traditional bread. "That's easy," he said without even thinking about it. "Cornbread." With that in mind here is a great recipe for some cornbread muffins.*

**2½ cups self-rising cornmeal**
**½ cup self-rising flour**
**2 eggs, beaten**

**¾ cups buttermilk**
**¼ cup honey**
**¼ cup sugar**

Combine all of the ingredients in a bowl and mix well. You can cook this recipe in a well-greased muffin pan, cornbread mold or even a bread loaf. This mix will rise so don't over fill. Bake in a 375° oven until golden brown.

## Deck Chef Tip!

### Perfect Pups

At a flea market in Chattanooga, Latrice and I struck up a conversation about cooking and her love for fried fish. I told her about my love for cornbread and hush puppies, so she gave me her secret for making perfectly round hush puppies. "I freeze the puppy batter and scoop it out with my fruit baller. Then I just drop them babies into the grease!" It works great! Now I make perfect ping-pong-size hush puppies each and every time.

# Hush Puppies

*I have had hush puppies served to me many times at many different restaurants that serve barbecue. Somehow it has become the perfect finger bread for a good plate of 'que. This recipe comes from T. L. who can't give his full name because he does not want his wife to know he gave out the recipe. Thanks T. L.—your secret is safe with us.*

3 cups self-rising cornmeal
1 cup self-rising flour
⅔ cup milk
¼ cup shredded Cheddar
  cheese

1 onion, chopped
1 teaspoon salt
1 teaspoon sugar
1 egg, beaten

Mix all into a cookie-like dough. Add or reduce milk as needed. Roll into balls or spoon into hot grease. Cook until outside is golden brown. Then serve hot.

# FIRE Hush Puppies

*Here is another simple recipe for hush puppies that will light your world on fire.*

3 cups self-rising cornmeal
1 cup self-rising flour
½ cup milk
½ cup beer
½ cup shredded pepper
  cheese
1 onion, chopped fine

2 eggs, beaten
⅓ cup diced jalapeño peppers
1 teaspoon crushed red pepper
1 teaspoon sugar
1 teaspoon minced garlic
Dash Cajun seasoning

Mix all, except the Cajun seasoning, into a thick dough. Add or reduce milk and beer as needed to achieve a cookie-dough-like consistency. Roll into balls and drop into hot grease; or spoon directly into hot grease. Cook until outside is golden brown. Oh yea, add a dash of Cajun seasoning right when the hush puppies come out of the fryer for added zest!

# Cook's BBQ

## 2929 Highway 41 • Ringgold, Georgia  30736
## (706) 965-5099

Cook's has been serving up great barbecue since 1958.  Located on scenic Highway 41—about 25 minutes from Chattanooga, Tennessee and about $1\frac{1}{2}$ hours North of Atlanta—Cook's is well worth the drive.  It is located in a small wooden building nestled in the bend of the road as you travel the Appalachian foothills.  Just off the front door and the parking lot sits a smokehouse that fills the nearby rolling hillsides with the smell of fresh barbecue.  "Some nights ya get so hungry when the smokers get going," a customer told me as we chatted outside.  "You know

sometime that day you're gonna come back and eat because you think about it all night and day long."

The menu items at Cook's starts with lunch and dinner plates.  Items include everything from slow- and low-cooked pork and beef to a half of chicken.  Not only do they load you up with a BUNCH of meat, each plate dinner comes with three side dishes and a thick chunk of Texas toast.  Cook's also sells bulk barbecue and complete family packs.

**GREAT EATS:**  I love ribs and Cook's does 'em good.  A friend of mine had the grilled cheese deluxe and it looked like one heck of a sandwich.

**NEAT THING:**  Cook's does a KILLER BREAKFAST that fills the parking lot before sunrise.  Try the Smoked Sausage Biscuit.

# North Georgia Apple Bread

*Not only is North Georgia known for beautiful mountains, wonderful small wineries and scenic golf, it is also a great place to find some of the tastiest apples ever grown. Submitted by D. Richards, North Georgia*

¾ cup sugar
¼ cup brown sugar
½ cup vegetable shortening
1 teaspoon vanilla
2 eggs, beaten

1 tablespoon butter, melted
1 tablespoon milk
2 cups sifted self-rising flour
1½ cups peeled, chopped
   apples

Mix both sugars, shortening and vanilla in a bowl with a mixer until fluffed. Stir in eggs, butter, milk and flour. Mix very well and then stir in the apples. When all is mixed well, pour into a well-greased cake pan. Spread the mixture until it is smooth on top.

**TOPPING:**
1 tablespoon sugar
1 tablespoon brown sugar

½ teaspoon cinnamon

Combine topping ingredients and sprinkle over batter. Bake 1 hour or until done in a 325° oven. You can serve this hot or cold.

# Country Sweet Potato Bread

*This is a nice twist on a bread recipe that uses the great taste of sweet potatoes. Beware, it uses a bunch of sugar, but it is worth it!*

2 cups firmly packed mashed
   sweet potatoes
2 cups white sugar
1 cup brown sugar
4 eggs, beaten
4 cups all-purpose flour

1 tablespoon baking soda
1 teaspoon salt
1 teaspoon ginger
1 teaspoon cinnamon
⅔ cup milk

Combine all ingredients in a large bowl and pour into a well-greased glass baking dish. Bake in a 350° oven for about 45 minutes and check. Cook an additional 15 minutes if needed. The bread will be firm in the center when done.

# West Virginia Blueberry Spoon Bread

*This recipe comes from the great state of West Virginia, thanks to Linda and Billy—"Smoky Bill," as he is known to his friends. Linda says that when blueberry season is over, frozen fruit works just as well.*

2 cups milk
1 teaspoon salt
1 teaspoon brown sugar
1 cup white cornmeal
2 cup self-rising flour

2 tablespoons butter
2 eggs, beaten
1 tablespoon sugar
1 cup fresh blueberries

In a saucepan combine milk, salt and brown sugar, and cook over low heat. When the mixture simmers, spoon in the cornmeal and flour until the mixture thickens. Remove from heat and spoon in butter, eggs, sugar and blueberries. You can add more flour or cornmeal to thicken or add a bit more milk to thin. Pour dough mixture into a well-greased bread pan or glass dish, and bake in the oven at 375° for about 25 to 30 minutes. Serve hot with a large spoon and some butter.

# Sweet Beer Bread

*I know, I can sneak a cold beer into just about any food group.*

4 cups self-rising flour
2 teaspoons sugar
1 tablespoon pancake syrup

½ teaspoon honey
2 eggs, beaten
2 (12-ounce) cans beer, divided

Mix all ingredients, except one beer, in a bowl. Place in greased bread pan and bake 55 minutes at about 350°. You can also cook it on a covered grill using high heat. Oh yeah, while the bread is baking, kick back and enjoy the second cold beer.

# So Simple Yeast Rolls

*One of the great things about eating at Kenny's house growing up were the yeast rolls his mom made. The smell of a batch of fresh yeast rolls coming out of the oven is a scent that makes eating carbohydrates worth it!*

**2¼ cups all-purpose flour**
**3 tablespoons sugar**
**1 teaspoon salt**
**1 pack dry active yeast**

**1 egg, beaten**
**2 large tablespoons shortening**
**Vegetable oil**

Combine flour, sugar, and salt. In a saucepan, boil 1 cup water; allow to cool until the bubbles stop, then add the yeast. Pour yeast mixture into flour mixture and add egg and shortening. Quickly mix all together well. Form the mix into a ball and rub with oil. Place in a large bowl, cover with cling-wrap and allow to rise for about an hour or until it has doubled in size. Break the dough into 10 equal pieces and form into balls; place balls into well-greased muffin pan. Cover very tightly with cling-wrap and allow the dough balls to rise again. Bake in a preheated 425° oven for about 15 minutes or until golden brown. Serve hot with a bit of butter.

**SO SIMPLE YEAST TWISTS**
Roll the dough balls into thin dough ropes. Take both ends and twist. You can roll them in cheese, butter, cinnamon or keep them plain.

## Deck Chef Tip!

### Rise and Shine

True yeast bread flavor comes from fermentation. Try to let your first fermentation period (rising) last at least an hour. Also, mix or work your dough as little as possible. If handled too much, it can become tough. Many people don't realize that flour can go bad. Store your flour in an airtight container to keep it as fresh as possible.

# Little Pigs BBQ

**1578 Hendersonville Road • Asheville, North Carolina  28803**
**(828) 2777188**

**100 Merrimon Avenue • Asheville, North Carolina  28801**
**(828) 253-4633**

**384 McDowell Street • Asheville, North Carolina  28803**
**(828) 254-4253**

There is a saying around Asheville, North Carolina . . . "The world famous Biltmore Estate came first . . . then came Little Pigs BBQ," or so the locals say.

Joe Swicegood opened Little Pigs in 1962 across from the high school in an old gas station down the road a bit from the main gates of Biltmore.  Today several locations around the Asheville area are operated by Carr Swicegood.

According to Rebecca Sams, the manager of Little Pigs BBQ on Hendersonville Road, they have had many famous guests.  Michael Jordan, Muhammad Ali, former President Jimmy Carter, and even the Reverend Billy Graham all have wiped barbecue sauce off their mouths there.

The original Little Pigs offers a down home, old-style barbecue joint with brick walls, huge black chalk boards with menu items, booths and tables scattered about.  The menu has something for everyone—pulled pork, ribs, combo plates, sandwiches and a full host of side items from slaw to tasty hush puppies.  When asked what made Little Pigs so good, Rebecca said the pork shoulders are slow-cooked in the pit for 15 hours.  "Just drive down the street late at night and you can smell the hickory in the air," she said.

**GREAT EATS:** Even though I am a barbecue freak, I still recommend you try the Crispy Chicken.  WONDERFUL!

**NEAT THING:**  Try some of the sauce.  Rebecca said they ship sauce to loyal out-of-town customers all the time.

# Kent's Hot Pepper Loaf

*I love spicy foods.  Here is a quick SPICY bread recipe that I love.*

2 cup self-rising flour
2 cups self-rising cornmeal
2 cups milk
2 eggs, beaten
½ cup sugar
¼ cup vegetable oil
1 stick butter, softened

1 cup shredded Cheddar cheese
½ cup chopped onion
½ cup chopped jalapeño pepper
1 teaspoon prepared horseradish
1 tablespoon minced garlic
1 teaspoon crushed red pepper

Combine all ingredients.  Place in a well-greased, well-floured bread pan.  Bake at 375° for about 40 minutes or until top is golden brown.

# Cheesy Ham Dinner Rolls

*I have had versions of this bread at several functions.  So here is a recipe that I consider a finger food, an appetizer, a bread and even a great snack.  And get this, it's simple!  Perfect for your next barbecue or tailgate party.*

2 packages store-bought dinner
    rolls in foil pans
10 to 12 slices honey ham
5 to 7 slices sandwich cheese
1 (8-ounce) package cream
    cheese, softened

1 teaspoon oregano
Allspice to taste
Salt and pepper to taste

Gently remove rolls from foil pans.  Slice rolls in half, so you have a top and a bottom.  Replace bottom half of rolls in foil pan.  Lay ham and cheese slices over bottom half rolls.  Spread a very thin layer of cream cheese on the top slices.  Sprinkle on a bit of oregano, allspice, salt and pepper.  Cover with the top half of rolls, and bake in a 350° oven until cheese is melted.  Serve hot.

# Grilled Biscuits

*This is a neat bread that can be cooked in an oven or on a grill that has a lid.*

2 cups self-rising flour
½ cup shredded jack cheese
¼ cup fine chopped ham
1 teaspoon salt

1¼ teaspoons confectioners'
  sugar
⅔ cup milk
⅓ cup vegetable oil

Combine flour, cheese, ham, salt and sugar; stir well. Add milk and oil, and mix until it forms a dough. Place dough on a lightly-floured surface and gently knead 8 or 10 times. Pat dough out to about ½-inch thick. Cut biscuits with a floured biscuit cutter. You can cook these babies in the oven at 400°, but I recommend that you put them in a foil pan right on the grill and close the lid. Cook until golden brown on top and serve hot.


# Grilled Olive Oil Pita Bread

Easy but a great finger bread for your next cookout. Buy a pack of pita bread and cut each piece in half. Brush a light coating of olive oil over each piece and grill directly over high heat for a few minutes on each side. For a bit of added zest, stuff a few pieces of onion slices, peppers, cheese or even barbecue into the hollow portion of the pita bread. I like to sprinkle a dash of parmesan cheese on the bread when still damp with olive oil.

# Coconut Cake Bread

*Man this stuff is great! It was hard to decide if this was a dessert or bread. But I finally decided on the bread section because it is cooked like a loaf. Plus, I'd eat it before, during and after any meal. It actually goes great with just about any recipe that includes jerk seasoning or anything spicy. Submitted by Jason S.*

2¼ cups self-rising flour
½ cup brown sugar
2 medium eggs, beaten
⅔ cup shredded coconut
4 tablespoons milk

1 teaspoon lemon juice
½ teaspoon vanilla flavoring
½ cup butter, softened
½ teaspoon salt
⅓ cup shredded coconut

Mix everything together in a bowl, except for the ⅓ cup coconut. Place in a well-greased loaf pan and bake at 325° for about 25 minutes. Remove from oven and top with remaining coconut. Cook an additional 5 to 10 minutes until coconut just begins to brown. This bread slices best when cooled. It is also great sliced and reheated with a bit of melted butter.

# Basic Banana Bread

*Here is a very simple recipe for making some great 'nanner bread.*

5 ripe bananas
4 eggs, beaten
1 cup shortening
2½ cups sugar
⅓ cup walnuts, optional

¼ cup brown sugar
1 tablespoon vanilla
3½ cups self-rising flour
1 teaspoon salt

Preheat oven to 300°. Mash bananas in a bowl and beat in eggs. In another bowl, combine remaining ingredients and mix. Add in Banana and egg mixture. Bake in two well-greased loaf pans for about an hour and 15 minutes. This recipe will make two good-sized loafs.

# John G's Bar-B-Q

**220 South Ocoee Street • Cleveland, Tennessee 37311**
**(423) 479-7885**

Located in a corner building in the heart of small town America, John G's Bar-B-Q often fills the sidewalks with the aroma of barbecue. After several careers that included jobs from computer programming to fire fighting, John DeArmond decided to turn his love for barbecue into a business.

The first John G's opened a few doors down from the current location. A few months after opening, John realized that his customers were overflowing onto the sidewalk. "It was time to look for a new place." After securing a building up the street, he spent nights renovating the larger location. One night when everything was ready, John, his crew and some friends spent the evening moving the whole restaurant up the sidewalk.

John G's walls are filled with all kinds of barbecue items. "About 99% of these things came from customers. I can honestly say I don't think I bought any of it," John said.

**GREAT EATS:** John will hand-grill you the biggest steak you've ever seen. "I have a smaller charcoal and wood chip grill I take out the back door on the sidewalk," says John. He then fires it up using a huge torch, and cooks the "perfect steak."

**NEAT THING:** John tells some great stories. Get him to tell you about the night the police called him after stopping a man walking down the street with several smoked butts stuffed in his clothes.

# Sides and Such

**Nothing makes a great barbecue or cookout like some fantastic side dishes.** One thing that always amazes me when I ask people about their favorite barbecue restaurants is after they tell me about the meat they always follow up with statements like this. "Man, and they have the best darned slaw in the world!" When you cook, eat and write about food and restaurants you discover that many have legendary side dishes that bring customers back as much as the main course. While the spotlight may shine brightly on the main course, the side stages are always filled with wonderful attractions. There are as many secret recipes for slaw and tater salad as there are for barbecue rubs. This section is dedicated to those wonderful dishes we simply call "Sides."

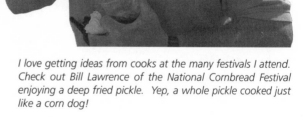

*I love getting ideas from cooks at the many festivals I attend. Check out Bill Lawrence of the National Cornbread Festival enjoying a deep fried pickle. Yep, a whole pickle cooked just like a corn dog!*

# Simple Coleslaw

*Here is a recipe for some very simple slaw to top your next barbecue sandwich.*

**1½ cups mayonnaise**
**½ cup white vinegar**
**¼ cup sugar**
**1 tablespoon celery salt**

**Salt and pepper to taste**
**1 head cabbage, shredded**
**2 carrots, shredded**

In a small bowl, blend mayonnaise, vinegar, sugar, celery salt and pepper. Mix well. Place cabbage and carrots in a large bowl and combine with the mixed ingredients. Cover and chill before serving. This slaw is perfect for topping a barbecue sandwich or as a side.

**Coleslaw is to barbecue what fireworks are on the Fourth of July.** I'm told that coleslaw has roots to both Asian and German styles of cooking. All I know is that some of the best barbecue sandwiches I have ever tasted were topped with some fresh, tasty coleslaw.

Many barbecue fans see coleslaw as a natural side dish to any decent barbecue plate. But where did coleslaw come from? Well, according to my barbecue pit master buddies, coleslaw may have been handed down from the heavens. While coleslaw can be as creamy and smooth as a star-filled sky, the real background has many paths. The general story is that coleslaw came into favor during the early 1900s when commercial mayonnaise came onto the market. It was an easy way to prepare shredded cabbage. Mustard-style coleslaw is often served during warmer months in parts of the South. Back in the early days, mustard slaw became popular because of lack of proper refrigeration.

# Easy Salad Oil Slaw

*This is a very easy recipe and is a great change of pace from mayo-based coleslaws.*

**2 pounds cabbage**
**1 cup salad oil**
**1/3 cup white vinegar**

**1 tablespoon garlic powder**
**1 teaspoon of salt**
**1 teaspoon black pepper**

Shred the cabbage and set aside in a large bowl. In a small bowl, mix the remaining ingredients and pour over the cabbage. Stir well. Add additional salt, pepper and garlic to suit your taste buds, if desired. Let it sit, covered, for a while in the fridge before serving.

# Country Buttermilk Coleslaw

*Back in the day, buttermilk was actually a by-product of the process used to make butter. Buttermilk is the residue milk skimmed off the top of the butter. The reason it is called buttermilk is that small pieces of butter could often be found in the milk. Today most buttermilk is mass-produced and the butter flavor is often added. I love this slaw. It is perfect for topping a massive hot dog, sausage or brat during a tailgate party.*

**1 pound cabbage, shredded**
**fine**
**2/3 cup chopped (very fine)**
**onion**
**1 carrot, chopped very fine**
**1 red pepper, chopped very fine**
**1/2 cup mayo**

**1/3 cup buttermilk**
**2 tablespoons cider vinegar**
**1 tablespoon sugar**
**1 teaspoon olive oil**
**1 teaspoon garlic powder**
**1 dash salt**
**1 dash pepper**

The secret to this slaw is making sure that the veggies are chopped into very fine pieces, so fine that they are almost minced. Mix all of the ingredients in a covered dish and store in the fridge as long as possible. Before serving, you can stir to incorporate the excess buttermilk that has drained to the bottom of the bowl, or actually drain some of it off.

# Perry's Bar-B-Q

**400 E. State Street • Black Mountain, North Carolina 28711**
**(828) 664-1446**

Several years back, Perry Cox moved from Austin, Texas, to Black Mountain, North Carolina. Like many others, he followed his dream to open a business that he loved . . . barbecue. Perry did what he did best, Texas-style barbecue—heavy on the beef and full of Southwestern flavor. While many found his barbecue a wonderful change of pace, many more asked for pork. Perry soon found his niche with a very nice blend of western North Carolina, eastern North Carolina, and of course, Texas-style barbecue. This combination of flavors makes his 'que a standout.

Perry's is based on the tried-and-true, Texas cafeteria-style buffet barbecue dinner. You walk in, point to what you want, and the server loads up your plate with huge, Texas-size portions.

Today Jack and Susan Spencer operate Perry's in line with the original dream. Expect huge portions, great sides, cold beverages and a smile. Because of local air pollution laws, Jack has an indoor smoker which uses hickory for flavor.

While you're in town, stop by the business district. The town is full of great shops and more. "It really has a Bohemian feel to it. Lots of neat places to go," Jack said.

**GREAT EATS:** Try the different sauces with your meal. When you are finished, dive head first into Susan's Banana Pudding and a chunk of Mississippi Mud Cake.

**NEAT THING:** After you get your plate, sit outside at a few small tables. The mountain breeze and the chance to wave at passing cars is pretty cool.

# Easy Red Cabbage Slaw

*This recipe takes full advantage of the beautiful color of red cabbage which can be added to any slaw recipe to make it more colorful.*

1 small green cabbage
1 small red cabbage
1 medium Vidalia onion, chopped
1 green bell pepper, chopped
⅔ cup cider vinegar
⅔ cup ketchup

1 cup oil
1 cup sugar
1 teaspoon dry mustard
1 teaspoon salt
½ teaspoon celery seeds
½ teaspoon pepper

The key to this slaw is the way I cut the cabbage. I slice or chop the cabbage into pieces that are about 3 inches long and as wide as a shoestring. Mix it with the chopped veggies in a big glass bowl. In a small saucepan, bring vinegar, ketchup, oil, sugar and spices to a boil until the sugar is dissolved. Remove from heat and let stand for a few minutes. Pour over veggies, cover and chill overnight. You can add some crushed red pepper for an added kick.

# Lee's Cajun-Style Hot Slaw

*Slaw is a great way to cool off a summer cook-out meal, but I enjoy spicy food so much that I'm always looking for a way to take dishes to the next level. Here is a great recipe given to me by my wife's grandmother, Lee.*

1 head cabbage, chopped
4 medium onions, chopped
5 hot green peppers, chopped
1½ cups white vinegar

½ cup water
¼ cup sugar
1 tablespoon crushed red pepper
Salt and pepper to taste

Toss cabbage, onion and hot peppers in a large bowl with lid. In a saucepan, combine white vinegar, water and sugar and boil for about 5 minutes. Allow to cool for a while and pour the liquid over the cabbage mixture. Top with the crushed red peppers, salt and pepper. Cover and chill until served.

# Festive Bell Pepper Slaw

*This slaw caught my eye—and my taste buds—the first time I tried it. It makes a great side dish, and if you are ever looking for a twist to a great Po-Boy sandwich, add this to your shrimp and French bread.*

¾ cup sugar
1 cup apple cider vinegar
2½ pounds cabbage
1 red pepper, chopped

1 green pepper, chopped
1 yellow pepper, chopped
½ tablespoon celery seed
Salt and pepper to taste

Mix sugar and vinegar and stir until sugar dissolves. Grate cabbage; chopped peppers, celery seed, salt and pepper. Pour sugar/vinegar mixture over cabbage mixture. Mix all well, cover and chill. As with many slaw recipes, the flavor will get better if covered and stored overnight.

## JAKE SAYS —

Be safe! Coleslaw and potato salad fall into the 60 minute rule—do not leave out more than 60 minutes without refrigeration.

# Lib's Grammy's German Potato Salad

*I don't know where Lib is from. I met her in Black Mountain, North Carolina. While waiting for a barbecue restaurant to open, I took in a few innings of a girl's softball tournament. Lib struck up a conversation by asking which young lady was my daughter. I told her about writing a barbecue book, and she told me her grandmother made the best potato salad ever. "Grammy came from Germany after the war when she was a little girl," Lib told me. "She made the best potato salad."*

About 12 red potatoes, sliced
8 slices bacon
1 medium onion, chopped
1 tablespoon all-purpose flour
½ cup water
¼ cup cider vinegar
1 tablespoon sugar
1 tablespoon mustard

½ teaspoon salt
⅛ teaspoon pepper
2 hard boiled eggs, chopped
¼ cup chopped celery
2 tablespoons chopped fresh
  parsley
Dash of minced garlic

Boil potatoes in water until done. While your potatoes are cooking, fry bacon in a skillet. Sauté onions in the drippings and slowly add flour and water, stirring continuously. Add the remaining ingredients and a bit of water if needed. Simmer for a few minutes. When the potatoes are done, remove them from the water and drain. Combine potatoes and sauce mixture in a large glass bowl. Stir well to make sure all potatoes are well coated. Add salt and pepper to taste if needed.

**Potato salad is a favorite at picnics.** There are two basic versions of potato salad—mayonnaise and mustard. It seems mustard potato salad originated back in the good old days when proper refrigeration was not available during the hot summer months. Some versions of mustard potato salads are also said to have German roots. Mayonnaise potato salad has a long history spanning back to the 18th century, but was made popular in the United States in 1912 by Richard Hellman. Hellman started canning his wife's favorite recipe at his factory, and introduced safe, store bought mayonnaise that could be used year round.

# Bacon & Potato Salad

*The first time I tried this dish, I was reminded of potato skins you can order at restaurants as an appetizer. This is easy, quick and a nice flavor-filled twist to potato salad.*

12 to 14 small red potatoes
½ cup ranch dressing
½ cup sour cream
½ cup shredded Cheddar
  cheese
½ cup shredded white jack
  cheese
1 cup cooked crumpled bacon
  (about 1 pound)

½ cup chopped celery stalk
1 small onion, finely chopped
2 small hard-boiled eggs,
  chopped
1 teaspoon garlic powder
Dash of crushed red pepper
Salt and pepper too taste

Wash the potatoes and dice them with the skin on into small pieces. Boil until fully cooked and remove from heat to cool. Mix all of the remaining ingredients in a large glass bowl. Cover and cool before serving.

# Mayo and Dijon Potato Salad

*Here is a quick version of the classic mayonnaise-based potato salad.*

5 to 6 medium baking
  potatoes, boiled
1 tablespoon apple cider
  vinegar
1 teaspoon sugar
½ cup chopped onion

3 tablespoons pickle relish
Salt and pepper to taste
⅔ cup mayonnaise
2 tablespoons Dijon mustard
1 hard-cooked egg, chopped

Peel and cube the boiled potatoes and put them in a medium bowl. Sprinkle with vinegar and sugar. Add onion, pickle relish, salt and pepper. Stir in mayonnaise until all of the potatoes are covered. Stir in Dijon mustard. Stir in your eggs last so they won't get too crushed. Cover and refrigerate for at least 1 hour before serving.

# Tangy Mustard Potato Salad

*Here is an easy-to-fix recipe for tangy potato salad. I actually use small baking potatoes for this recipe, but red potatoes would work as well.*

5 small baking potatoes, diced
  and cooked
½ cup diced celery
¼ cup chopped onion
2 tablespoons parsley
½ tablespoon apple cider
  vinegar

2 tablespoons Dijon Mustard
1 tablespoon mustard
1 teaspoon hot sauce (optional)
Salt and pepper to taste
1 tablespoon sour cream
  (more if desired)

Combine all ingredients except the sour cream. Toss lightly and chill for a while to soak up the flavor. A few hours before serving time, stir in the sour cream to make it creamy.

## Deck Chef Tip!

### Tater Tip

Small red or waxy potatoes are great for making potato salad. Red potato skins are thinner and easier to clean. The skin is also easier to chew, making it unnecessary to peel them before using. Talk about a time saver! The color of the skin of red potatoes adds a nice touch to potato salad.

Red potatoes are lower in starch than baking potatoes. To test a potato for its starch content, place the tater in water. If it floats, it's a low starch or wax potato. If it sinks, then it is a high starch potato or baking potato. Baking potatoes are perfect for baking and making mashed potatoes because they have large amounts of starch to soak up the butter and sour cream.

# Carolina Smokehouse

**U.S. Highway 64W • Cashiers, North Carolina 28717**
**(828) 743-3200**

Somewhere between the North Carolina, South Carolina and North Georgia mountains lies Cashiers, North Carolina, offering beautiful mountains in every direction as well as some great golf resorts. Just as you drive down Highway 64W on one of the few straight pieces of asphalt, you will see Carolina Smokehouse.

Carolina Smokehouse has a great history and some great 'que. During my stop there, I talked with Rachael, visited with some customers, got a tour of the smoke-house, and of course ate a great meal. According to Rachael, the place started many years ago as a mountain restaurant.

Today, Rob and Tammy Williams are the owners of this fantastic barbecue restaurant which offers a huge indoor dining room and a large porch filled with tables perfect for eating some Carolina Smokehouse 'que.

During the smokehouse tour, my guide hinted at several things that make the barbecue great at Carolina Smokehouse—quality meat, unique seasonings, SLOW cooking and a simple menu that still offers something for everyone.

**GREAT EATS:** Are you really hungry? Try "The Pit Combo." It's a platter filled with barbecue ribs, beef, pork and chicken—all lip-smacking good. And, of course, you get heaping sides of slaw, fries, Texas toast and even some soup with a nice piece of cornbread.

**NEAT THING:** If the weather is nice, sit outside.

# Tex-Mex Tater Salad

*I'm a sucker for traditional barbecue sides, but I know a good thing when I taste it. This festive version of potato salad has the flavor of the Southwest.*

8 russet potatoes, peeled and cubed
1½ cups shredded Cheddar cheese
⅔ cup black beans, rinsed and drained
⅔ cup chopped red bell pepper

1½ cups chopped celery
1⅓ cups chopped green onions
1 tablespoon cilantro (or parsley)
2 cups sour cream
½ cup ranch dressing
1½ cups medium chunky salsa
Salt and pepper to taste

In a large bowl, combine the potatoes, cheese, beans, bell pepper, celery, onions and cilantro.  In a small bowl, combine sour cream, salad dressing, salsa, salt and pepper.  Pour sauce over potato mixture and toss to coat.  Cover and refrigerate for at least 1 hour.  For some more heat, add a touch of cumin powder, crushed red pepper and a dash of garlic.

## Deck Chef Tip!

### Dare to Be Different!

Looking to make a boring potato salad a bit different?  Here are some neat ideas to boost the flavor of your favorite potato salad.  Try adding chopped nuts such as almonds or pecans. Spice it up with some hot sauce or horseradish. Add bacon, lemon zest, carrots, diced peppers, garlic and more.  Even some fresh diced fruit or a handful of raisins can be added.

# So Dang Simple Baked Beans

*The simplest recipe for baked beans is open the can and pour in bowl. If you are ready to jump that up a bit, here is a very easy recipe.*

**2 cans pork and beans**
**1 onion, chopped fine**
**½ cup brown sugar**

**¼ cup mustard**
**¼ cup ketchup**

Combine all ingredients in a glass baking dish. Bake in a 275° oven for two hours or more.

## JAKE SAYS —

Try adding a spoonful of your favorite jelly or jam to your next batch of baked beans. Don't add too much or your beans might taste like breakfast!

# Sausage and Baked Beans

**½ pound sausage**
**2 cans pork and beans**
**½ cup diced tomatoes**
**¼ cup brown sugar**
**1 green pepper, chopped**
**¼ ginger ale**
**1 large onion, chopped**

Cook sausage in skillet like ground beef (not in slices). Combine sausage with other ingredients in a covered glass baking dish. Bake for 1 hour at 350°.

# Fire Baked Beans

*Warn your guests. These beans may be a bit spicy! Be very careful not to get pepper juice in your eyes when cutting.*

2 cans pork and beans
1 can black beans
1 onion, diced
1 bell pepper, diced
1 banana pepper, diced

⅓ cup chopped jalapeño
  peppers with juice
½ cup brown sugar
¼ cup whiskey
¼ pound raw bacon

Combine all (except bacon) and place in a glass cooking dish. Lay bacon on top. Cook at 350° for about 1 hour, then reduce heat to 200° and continue to cook off the extra juice. You may want to cover very loosely with foil.

# Three-Bean Baked Beans

*Using more than one type of bean in a baked bean recipe will make for a great look, texture and TASTE!*

1 large onion, chopped fine
¼ cup extra virgin olive oil
1 tablespoon minced garlic
1 can baked beans
1 can kidney beans

1 can pinto beans
½ cup finely diced tomatoes
¼ cup brown sugar
¼ cup beer
4 bacon strips

Add everything to a glass baking dish. Stir well and cover loosely with foil. Bake at 275° for two hours or more. About halfway through the cooking process, place the bacon on top of the beans. Return to oven, uncovered, for the remaining cooking time. While the beans are cooking, you can sip on the remainder of the beer.

# Bacon and Apple Baked Beans

*This recipe comes from the beautiful North Georgia Mountains which are dotted with apple orchards.*

2 (16-ounce) cans pork and
  beans
½ cup chopped onion
⅓ cup chopped apples
1 can tomato paste

½ cup barbecue sauce
¼ cup brown sugar
¼ cup golden raisins
8 bacon strips

Drain pork and beans and place into a glass dish. Add onion and apples; stir. Add tomato paste, barbecue sauce, brown sugar and raisins. Mix well and lay bacon strips on top. Place in oven and bake at 300° for 2 to 3 hours.

# Tex-Mex Baked Beans

1 hot banana pepper, diced
1 red bell pepper, diced
1 medium onion, diced
2 garlic cloves, minced
1 tablespoon olive oil
1 can chicken broth
½ tablespoon cumin
1 can black beans

1 can pork and beans
1 can whole kernel corn
1 small can diced tomatoes
  and green chilies
1 tablespoon chili powder
½ teaspoon garlic
½ tablespoon hot sauce
1 tablespoon apple vinegar

In a large skillet, brown the peppers, onion, and garlic in oil for 3 minutes. Stir in broth and cumin. Bring to a boil. Reduce heat, cover and simmer for 15 minutes. Add remaining ingredients; heat and serve.

# Molasses (Boston) Baked Beans

*I have tasted many Boston Baked Bean recipes and I love this version because of the cinnamon and molasses. This recipe comes from Mrs. T. Johnson. She says it takes a long time to cook 'em, but it's worth it.*

½ **pound pea beans**
½ **pound kidney beans**
1 **tablespoon mustard**
1 **teaspoon salt**
¼ **teaspoon pepper**
2 **onions, quartered**

¼ **cup brown sugar**
¼ **cup molasses**
2 **tablespoons vinegar**
1 **teaspoon cinnamon**
1 **teaspoon garlic powder**
¼ **pound salt pork**

Pick over beans and wash. Cover with 3 cups water and soak 8 hours or overnight. Drain and rinse the soaked beans. Add 2 cups water, mustard, and the rest of the ingredients except salt pork. Boil, covered, about 1 hour or until skins start to wrinkle. Heat oven to 300°. Cut salt pork into cubes and place in a glass dish. Pour beans over. Sprinkle with additional pepper and bake, covered, for 6 hours or until tender. When beans are two-thirds cooked, pour a few tablespoons water over the top and cook uncovered for last 30 minutes.

## Deck Chef Tip!

### Low and Slow

Baked beans can have all different kinds of ingredients. The trick to good baked beans is to cook them low and slow like barbecue. Loosely cover the dish with foil, cook in a low oven, and let much of the moisture cook off. If using bacon on top, uncover for the last 30 minutes or so to crisp the bacon.

# Bandana's Bar B Que & Grill

**1475 Highway 105 • Boone, North Carolina 28607**
**(828) 265-2828**

Bandana's Bar B Que and Grill is located in the beautiful Mountains of Boone, North Carolina. They offer great tasting barbecue in a wide open, family environment.

The food is great. The menu is packed with everything from barbecue to huge steaks to salads and shrimp. Their claim to fame is their mouth-watering ribs. "People love our ribs. They can get them full rack, half, or baby back—eat-in or to-go," says Mary.

According to the crew at Bandana's, the secret to their barbecue is a time-honored barbecue tradition. "We use only hickory to smoke all of our meats," Mary said. We had a large pit inside, but we moved it to the other side and converted the old pit into a large grill where we grill HUGE Buckhead Beef Steaks. People love watching the fire and the steaks being grilled."

**GREAT EATS:** Their baby back ribs, steaks, and smoked turkey are all delicious. For fun, try the massive barbecue cheese fries. They also have a great kids' menu.

**NEAT THING:** Check out the grill up front. Nothing beats that great steak smell. Also, take a minute to check out the auto tags around the restaurant and count the states.

# Southern White Beans

*Jamie Whitaker swears that a good bowl of white beans puts all other Southern cooking to shame. Believe it or not, white beans are easy to prepare. As any good Southern Belle would tell you, there are two ways to measure beans . . . enough for when folk are coming over, and enough for when folk are not coming over. Here is the recipe for when folks are coming over.*

**1 (2-pound) bag white beans**　　**1 teaspoon minced garlic**
**1 left-over ham bone**　　　　　**½ teaspoon black pepper**
**1 onion, chopped**　　　　　　　**Salt to taste**

First, sort your beans and remove any rocks or bad beans. Soak the remaining beans (in water to cover) overnight in a large pan. Use a large pan because the beans will double in size and overflow in one that is too small. Rinse the soaked beans with warm water and return to large pan. Add water to cover and remaining ingredients. Cook over high heat until they boil, and then turn the heat down as low as it can go and cook until done (or until you can't stand to smell them one more minute without eating).

## Deck Chef Tip!

### 'Dem Bones

Every time we cook a ham, Jamie can't wait to get the ham bone so she can seal it in a freezer bag for the next time she makes white beans. "There is no exact science to making white beans," she says. "The key is to leave them alone as much as possible. Don't let them dry out and don't let them burn, but don't overstir the beans. Cook as low and slow as possible."

# Simple Grilled Veggies

*Grilling veggies over hot coals is a no brainer. Many people make it harder than it is. Here are a couple of simple items that will make you look like a grill master with vegetables.*

## Onions

Buy sweet onions and slice them into quarter-inch slices and douse with vinegar. Add a dash of garlic powder and maybe a bit of ginger then toss them on the grill. Grill the onions in complete ring slices like a burger.

## Asparagus

Brush with extra virgin olive oil, dash with a bit of salt and pepper. Place them on the grill and cook like a hot dog over high heat.

## Zucchini

Zucchini can be cooked like the asparagus. Or you can brush with soy sauce, brown sugar and ginger.

## Tomatoes

Slice the tomatoes into thick slices. Brush with extra virgin olive oil and add a dash of salt and a dash of allspice. Grill and turn to bubble the skin on the tomato.

## Foil Packs

Make or buy those foil packs and stuff them with all kinds of fresh-cut veggies. Add some butter, pepper, salt and a few drops of water. Close the pack and toss it on the grill while you are cooking other items. When the main dish is done, pull off the foil pack and open it for some great steamed veggies.

# Vinaigrette Grilled Vegetables

*Besides your normal veggies, try some eggplant, mushrooms and thin-sliced corn on the cob with this recipe.*

**4 cups cut-up assorted
  vegetables**
**½ cup vinaigrette dressing**

**Dash sage**
**Salt and pepper to taste**

Combine vegetables, dressing, sage, salt and pepper in a large zip-close plastic bag.  Place in the fridge for an hour or more.  Remove the veggies from the bag, and place on the grill over medium to medium-high heat.  If needed, use a veggie basket for the grill or a layer of foil.  Grill for about 10 to 20 minutes, depending on how crisp you like them.  You can brush with leftover dressing, and sprinkle with a light coating of the allspice as soon as you remove them from the grill.  Serve hot.

# Melissa's Taters

*Melissa is one of the funniest people I have ever met.  She also has great, easy recipes.  Here is one that makes a yummy potato dish with out having to cut a bunch of "Taters."*

**1 bag frozen hash browns**
**2 cans cream of chicken soup**

**1 cup sour cream**
**1 cup shredded cheese**

**TOPPING:**
**Crushed Ritz crackers**

**2 tablespoons butter, melted**

In large bowl, mix hash browns, soup, sour cream, and cheese and place in greased cake-size pan.  Cook at 350° for 45 minutes.  Remove from oven and add Topping (crushed Ritz crackers mixed with butter) then cook for 15 minutes more.

# Jon's Leftover French Fries

*This recipe came to me from barbecue junkie Jon. He swears this is the best way to get rid of leftover baked potatoes. Submitted by Jon from Hastings, MN (note: not Appalachian!!)*

**6 potatoes, baked**  **Salt and pepper**
**Cajun seasoning**

Take completely cooled baked potatoes and slice them into large "steak fries." Fry in hot oil and sprinkle with Cajun seasoning, salt and pepper. As Jon says "The perfect French fry. Absolutely the crispiest, best fries ever! Yummy!"


# Whole Baked Sweet Potatoes

*Here is an easy way to serve baked potatoes with a simple butter topping. Check out my bud Tom's idea at the end of the recipe.*

**Fresh sweet potatoes**  **1 tablespoon honey**
**1 stick butter, melted**  **1 teaspoon brown sugar**

Just poke a few holes in your washed sweet potatoes and wrap them in some foil. Toss them in the oven and cook until you can poke them with a fork. While your sweet taters are cooking, mix butter, honey and brown sugar together. Top your taters while they're hot.

Looking for sweet taters on the grill? Cut sweet potatoes in half, coat with some oil and wrap in foil a few times. Toss your foil-wrapped sweet potatoes directly onto the coals. Remove when soft, and eat. Or, if you have some time, let the sweet potatoes cool, slice them into huge fries and coat them with some butter with brown sugar. Then grill them over hot coals.

# Green Tomatoes

*Slice 'em, dip 'em, coat 'em and fry 'em.*

**3 green tomatoes, sliced**
  **½-inch thick**
**2 eggs, beaten**

**½ cup cornmeal**
**Salt and pepper**

Dip tomatoes in the egg, then in a mixture of cornmeal, salt and pepper. Fry in hot oil until golden brown. This will make a crisp-fried green tomato.

    For a different taste, toss them on the grill over wood chips for a few minutes. Place a sheet of foil over the grates and spray it with non-stick spray before starting the grill. Once the grill is hot, place the dipped tomatoes onto the foil over high heat. Cook and turn. This will make a softer green tomato. Enjoy!

# Bob's French Tomato Salad

*While in the service, my Uncle Bob spent many years in France. He lived in a small boarding house and became very good friends with the family who ran it. This was one of his favorite dishes while staying there.*

**4 cloves garlic, bruised**
**5 medium-size fresh tomatoes**
**½ cup extra virgin olive oil**
**½ cup red wine vinegar**
**¼ cup chopped shallots**

**3 tablespoons parsley**
**2 tablespoons fresh tarragon**
**1 large dash salt**
**1 large dash pepper**

Rub a shallow glass dish with the garlic. Slice tomatoes stem end to bud end and arrange in a domino fashion in the dish. Mix olive oil and vinegar and gently pour over tomatoes. Sprinkle with shallots, parsley, tarragon, salt and pepper. Cover with cling wrap and let stand at least 2 hours. According to Bob, feel free to add extra shallots, parsley or whatever. The key is to let it rest so the tomatoes soak up the flavor. Depending on the depth of your dish, you may need to baste often.

# Turpins BBQ

## 2055 N. Highway 25 • Travelers Rest, South Carolina 29690
## (864) 834-8737

**B**ack in the late '60s, Turpins Roadside Restaurant served up great burgers, fries, veggies and Southern cooking to hungry drivers heading back and forth between North Carolina and South Carolina. Today Turpins, located a few minutes outside of Greenville, South Carolina, serves up great barbecue. Dawanna

Pickelsimer, daughter of owners Gail and John Griffith, says since her parents have owned Turpins, the menu has slowly changed. According to Dawanna, John started cooking barbecue and added it to the menu. "Next thing you know, we were a barbecue restaurant!"

About the only thing from the old menu is the Turpin Burger which is huge and covered in chili, cheese, bacon, onion, lettuce, tomatoes and more! Today, their menu also offers pulled pork, ribs, shrimp, chopped chicken, sides such as homemade potato chips, and a massive barbecue baked potato. Before you enter

Turpins, take a look to the right and check out the smoke pouring from the pits!

**GREAT EATS:** After your meal, try the Apple Tortilla Flip created by Dawanna's mom. It's a big fried tortilla filled with apple, cinnamon, ice cream and more. Very good!

**NEAT THING:** The walls, shelves, ceiling and parts of the floor are covered with the largest collection of barbecue pig items I have ever seen. You could spend hours looking at it all.

# Green Bean & Corn Casserole

*Bruce C. says you must use shoe peg corn in this recipe—no substitutes!*

2 cups crushed Ritz-type
  crackers, divided
2 (14-ounce) cans French-style
  green beans, drained
1 (14-ounce) can shoe peg corn
1 can sliced water chestnuts

1 small onion, finely chopped
1 (14-ounce) can cream of
  celery soup
8 ounces sour cream
1 cup shredded Cheddar cheese
1 stick butter, melted

Layer ½ cup crackers, beans, corn, water chestnuts, and onion in a greased 9x13-inch pan. Combine soup, sour cream, cheese, and butter a small bowl and pour over mixture in pan. Top with remaining 1½ cups crackers (and chopped almonds, if desired). Bake in the oven at 350° for 30 to 35 minutes.

# Corn Pudding

*A traditional side dish around every cookout in this family.*

3 eggs, beaten
3 tablespoons sugar
1 tablespoon brown sugar
1 large dash salt

1 large dash black pepper
½ cup butter, melted
2 cans creamed corn

Mix all in glass baking dish and cook in a 300° oven for about 30 or 40 minutes.

# Baked Corn Casserole

2 cans whole kernel corn
1 (5-ounce) box seasoned rice
1 stick butter, melted
1 can cream of mushroom soup

½ loaf processed American
  cheese
1 cup hot salsa
½ cup chopped onion

Mix all ingredients and bake at 350° for about 30 minutes. You can top with more cheese of your choice, if desired.

# Jamie's Fried Corn

*Jamie's recipe for fried corn is simple. The minimal amount of ingredients really makes the flavor of the corn stand out.*

4 to 6 ears silver queen corn
½ cup half-and-half
1 teaspoon chili powder
1 teaspoon allspice

1 large dash salt and pepper
1 large dash crushed red pepper
⅓ cup chopped onion

Slice the corn off the cob and rub the dull end of the knife across the cob to coax out the juice. Combine all ingredients in a skillet and simmer until most of the moisture is cooked off. You can add more spices as needed to make this recipe really spicy.

# Fried Corn on the Cob

*I have to admit that when I first tried this recipe I was unsure about the flavor, so I decided that the corn needed a bit more POP! As any good, heat-loving deck chef would do, I added some spices to the original recipe. The easy way to think of this recipe is corn on a stick like a corn dog. Submitted By Bruce C.*

1 large egg, beaten
½ cup milk
2 tablespoons hot sauce
1 cube chicken bouillon
½ cup all-purpose flour

1 teaspoon chili powder
1 teaspoon allspice
1 large dash garlic
1 large dash salt and pepper
4 ears corn on cob

Combine egg, milk, hot sauce and bouillon in a bowl. Stir well and make sure cube is completely dissolved. Add flour, chili powder, all-spice, garlic, salt and pepper. Get your deepest skillet or deep fryer ready and HOT. Cut the ears of corn in half and dip each piece in the mixture. Deep fry the coated corn in hot oil until golden brown. If you can find some sticks like those used in corn dogs, pick up a few packs. Drain the finished fried corn on some paper towels and serve hot! Bruce also says you can keep the wet and dry ingredients separate and dip the corn in the wet and then roll in the dry for a different texture. Just reduce the amount of milk used.

# Fried Okra

*Okra is a dish loved by many and dreaded by just as many. If you like okra, this is a great recipe that is very easy.*

**1 pound small okra pods**
**¾ cup cornmeal**
**1 tablespoon allspice**

**Salt and pepper**
**Bacon Fat**

Wash okra and cut off the ends of the pods, slice to ½-inch thick. Moisten slightly and shake in paper bag containing cornmeal, allspice, salt, and pepper. Fry in hot bacon fat until breading around okra is golden brown.

# The Ultimate Mac and Cheese

*This recipe is dedicated to my son who is a mac and cheese freak. Actually, now he loves pasta shells and cheese. Anyway, the more cheese and flavor, the better.*

**2 cups elbow macaroni (or shells), cooked just shy of "done"**
**4 tablespoons butter, divided**
**¼ cup self-rising flour**
**1 cup milk**
**1 pound processed American cheese, cut into chunks**

**1 cup shredded Cheddar cheese, divided**
**½ cup finely chopped cooked bacon or ham**
**¼ cup crushed Ritz-style crackers**

Melt butter in a medium saucepan on very low heat. Add flour and stir well to mix. Cook and stir until the mixture begins to bubble and thicken. Add milk slowly, stirring until well blended. Add process cheese and ½ cup Cheddar cheese; cook until melted, stirring frequently. Stir in macaroni and bacon or ham; pour into a lightly buttered glass baking dish. Melt 1 tablespoon butter, add remaining cheese and cracker crumbs, and place on top. Bake for about 30 minutes at 350° or until crackers are golden brown.

# Morrison's Barbecue

**13200 Highway 225 North • Crandall, Georgia 30711**
**(706) 517-5424**

In 1929, Dr. T. W. Colvard built a small country store in the shadows of the North Georgia Mountains. According to current building and restaurant owners, Robin and Larry Morrison, the store was built to give the good doctor's daughters something to do.

Today, when you open the screened front door, you quickly step back in time. The floors creak, the beautiful tables and chairs fill a room lined with the original shelves used to hold the store's goods. Today those shelves hold antiques—some for sale, some for looking. The walls are lined with kids' drawings on construction paper.

**GREAT EATS:** Morrison's serves up everything from pulled pork, beef and chicken, to great steaks and even shrimp. Kids will enjoy burgers, "Dawgs," and more. You may want to try the smoked turkey salad or the Brunswick stew and a whole host of sides and desserts.

**NEAT THING:** Morrison's will smoke your own cuts of meat for a very low price. "Around a buck a pound," Robin said.

# Desserts

**Nothing tops off a great barbecue or cookout like a fantastic dessert.** Sure, the county fair always has some great barbecue, burgers and dogs, but take a look at the bake sale area . . . table after table of mouth-watering, sweet desserts!

Don't think banana pudding is the only thing you can eat for dessert when eating a big pulled barbecue sandwich. These recipes come from people who love the smoked flavor of barbecue but have a big sweet tooth as well.

**Want to get a funny look?** Ask a watermelon producer where the watermelon came from. "My farm." Once we got past that, I found out that watermelons are actually a dessert fruit that may have originated in Africa and are about 92% water. I was told once that if you eat too many watermelon seeds that a melon would grow in your stomach. "Not true," according to the farmer I quizzed. He says every bit of a watermelon can be eaten, even the rind.

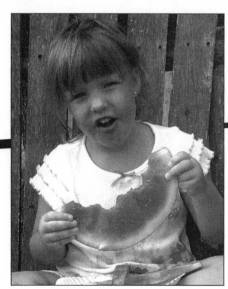

# Uh-Oh Nanny's Pound Cake

2 sticks butter
3 cups sugar
6 large eggs, beaten
3 cups self-rising flour

1 cup milk
2 tablespoons spiced rum
2 teaspoons lemon flavoring
1 teaspoon almond flavoring

The secret according to Uh-Oh Nanny's Pound Cake is to start this cake out in a cold oven. Grease and flour a tube pan (you know, the pound cake pan with a hole). In a large bowl, cream your butter and sugar and add eggs one at a time. Add the flour and milk slowly. "A bit of flour, stir. A bit of milk, stir. A bit of flour, stir." When all is mixed well, add the spiced rum, lemon flavoring, and almond flavoring, and stir them in. Pour your cake mix into the greased and floured pan and place it in the oven. Set your oven for 325° and bake for about one hour. Check the cake with a toothpick. If the top starts to brown, just the cover the cake with foil. Total cooking time is around 1 hour and 15 minutes.

My wife's grandmother, Lee Kellet, called one night on her cordless to tell my wife she fell down the stairs and the ambulance was coming. We only lived a few doors down so my wife packed my son Macee, then two years old, in his car seat and they zoomed up the street. Grandmother had slipped down the stairs and broken a leg. I was at work at the time but everyone swears that when Macee saw his great grandmother, Nanny, sitting there at the bottom of the stairs with firefighters and medics, he raised his hand up and said, "Uh-oh Nanny." Uh-oh was the word we all said when Macee fell or dropped food on his bib. Ever since then my son has called his great grandmother "Uh-Oh Nanny."

# Kent's Spiced Rum Cake

**RUM CAKE:**

½ cup chopped pecans
½ cup chopped walnuts
1 box yellow cake mix
1 box instant vanilla pudding

3 eggs
½ cup water
⅓ cup oil
⅓ cup spiced rum

**GLAZE:**

⅓ stick butter, softened
¼ cup water
½ cup brown sugar

⅓ cup sugar
⅓ cup spiced rum

Preheat oven to 325°. Place mixed nuts in bottom of a well-greased 12-inch Bundt cake pan. Mix remaining cake ingredients together and gently pour over nuts. Bake for about 1 hour or until a toothpick inserted in the middle comes out clean. When done, remove from oven and allow the cake to cool.

Mix all glaze ingredients together and warm in microwave until butter melts. Mix well. Remove cake from pan and coat with glaze. Top each slice with a bit of whipped cream when serving.

# Sorghum Carrot Cake

**CAKE:**

1½ cups cooking oil
4 eggs
2 tablespoons soda
¼ tablespoon salt

2 cups sugar
2 cups cake flour
2 tablespoons cinnamon
3 cups grated cheese

**FILLING:**

1 stick margarine
1 cup chopped nuts
1 (8-ounce) package cream
  cheese

2 tablespoons vanilla
2 cups powdered sugar
⅓ cups sorghum

Combine all cake ingredients and pour evenly into 2 round greased cake pans. Cook in 350° oven for about 25 to 30 minutes. Let cool before removing from pan.

Combine Filling ingredients and spread evenly between the two layers. Top with a few extra chopped nuts.

# Speedy Lohr's Barbecue

**8000 Highway 150 North • Arcadia, North Carolina 27295**
**(336) 764-5509**

**10774 Highway 8 South • Southmont, North Carolina 27351**
**(336) 798-1538**

Roger Lohr carries on the tradition of being a barbecue pit master and restaurant owner that his father started back in 1963. His restaurant, Speedy Lohr's, is located just outside of Lexington, North Carolina, in Arcadia. "My dad, Sherman Paul Lohr, or Speedy, taught me at his place from 1963 to about 1970. Then we were at our Southmont location until 1989, when I opened my restaurant in Arcadia," Roger said.

Roger says his style of barbecue is considered Lexington style. Without giving away any secrets, Roger gave out a few ingredients during our conversations. "Vinegar, salt, pepper . . . some water."

**GREAT EATS:** People come from miles around to munch on Speedy Lohr Skins. "We take the skins from our pork shoulders and season them up a bit. We then cook them in a deep fryer at about 350 degrees for about 10 minutes or until the bubbles stop. We serve them hot with our signature barbecue dip or our hot sauce."

# Nell's Loaf Cake

*Mrs. Rutledge lived next door to my Mom and Dad in Nashville when I was growing up. My brothers and I were only a short walk through the track of trees and across the log bridge crossing the small creek to her house. This is the recipe Nell gave my mom for her famous Loaf Cake before she passed away.*

**CAKE:**

1 box butter cake mix
1 box instant vanilla pudding
4 eggs, beaten
¾ cup water

¾ cup oil
1 teaspoon butter flavoring
1 teaspoon vanilla flavoring

**FILLING:**

½ cup sugar
4 tablespoons cinnamon

½ cup chopped pecans

Combine and mix all cake ingredients. Set aside. Combine and mix filling ingredients and set aside. Grease and flour a bundt cake pan. First spoon in a small amount of the filling. Then a layer of the cake mix. Then a few spoonfuls of filling. Then a layer of cake mix. You can make more filling if desired. Bake in a 350° oven for about 45 to 60 minutes. Check often.

*Wes, B.J., and Ashton enjoy outdoor cooking all year 'round.*

# Double Cola Cake

*The home of Double Cola is located in Chattanooga, Tennessee. Double Cola was born around 1922 and has been a staple around the South ever since. I first tried a Double Cola cake at a small-town fair somewhere and have looked for a recipe ever since. This is what I have come up with by trying several versions.*

**CAKE:**

2 cups all-purpose flour
2 cups sugar
3 tablespoons cocoa
1 cup Double Cola
1½ cups miniature
 marshmallows

1 cup butter
2 eggs, beaten
½ cup buttermilk
1 teaspoon baking soda
1 teaspoon vanilla extract

**FROSTING:**

½ cup butter
1 tablespoon cocoa
6 tablespoons Double Cola

1 (1-pound) box confectioners'
 sugar
½ cup chopped pecans

Grease and flour a 9 x 13-inch pan and set aside. In a large bowl, combine flour and sugar and mix well. In a medium-size saucepan, combine cocoa, Double Cola, marshmallows and butter, and very slowly bring the mixture to a boil. Combine the boiled mixture with the flour and sugar mixture. Mix in eggs, buttermilk, baking soda, and vanilla. Make sure everything is well blended, and then pour the mixture into a prepared pan and bake at 350° for about 35 to 40 minutes until cake tests done. Remove from oven and let cool while you prepare your frosting.

In a saucepan, bring butter, cocoa, and Double Cola to a boil. Stir in the sugar and mix well. Stir in nuts. Remove frosting from heat. Take the round end of a small wooden spoon and poke holes into the cake about every two inches. Before the frosting cools, spread it over the cake. Serve warm or cold.

# Mountain Dew Cake

*This is a great cake with a nice flavor from one of my favorite sodas. As many of my friends know, a Mountain Dew is by my side on many a late night smoke session. Here is a cake recipe dedicated to my overnight pork smoking "go go juice" (as my niece calls it).*

**2 sticks margarine, melted**
**5 large eggs**
**½ cup shortening, softened**
**1 teaspoon lemon extract**

**3 cups sugar**
**3½ cups flour**
**1 can Mountain Dew**

Mix all ingredients except Mountain Dew. Blend them all well before adding Mountain Dew. Add about ½ can and stir in. Add more as needed to make cake batter. If you don't need the whole can, then don't use it. Pour your cake batter in a well-greased rectangle cake pan or greased glass cake dish. Bake in 300° oven for about 1 hour or until done. Top with your favorite icing or whipped cream.

## JAKE SAYS —

If you can't get your hands on a Double Cola, then try your favorite brand or flavor. Root beer is good in dark cakes.

# Granny Hazel's Strawberry Cake

**CAKE:**

1 package white cake mix
1 package instant strawberry
  jello
1 cup oil

½ cup boiled water
4 eggs
½ cup crushed strawberries

**ICING:**

½ stick margarine, melted
1 cup confectioners' sugar

½ cup crushed strawberries

Combine cake ingredients and mix with a blender on medium speed for about 4 minutes. Bake the cake in a greased and floured pan at 350°. Cook until firm in the center, about 25 to 30 minutes.

For the icing, mix the melted margarine, sugar and strawberries. The icing will be a bit runny but it will set up when chilled in the fridge.

# Easy Strawberry Delight

*Thanks for the recipe, H.W. As you asked, I am passing it on to your neighbors. This is really easy to make and requires no baking.*

1 store-bought angel food cake
2 packages strawberry jello
1 (20-ounce) package frozen
  strawberries, thawed

2 cups milk
1 box vanilla pudding
8 ounces whipped cream

Cut cake into slices and arrange onto the bottom of a glass baking dish. Make strawberry Jello in a large bowl by following the directions on the box; stir in the strawberries. Pour over the cake slices and place in the fridge. While in the fridge, make your pudding and gently spoon over the set Jello. When the pudding sets, cover with whipped cream. Serve cold and garnish with fresh strawberries.

# THE HISTORY OF THE GREAT AMERICAN MOONPIE

Just about anybody that has ever been in the South has had a MoonPie®! This handful of graham crackers with marshmallow filling dipped in rich chocolate is a staple for snack lovers looking for something filling. In fact, according to my friends at the Chattanooga Bakery, which was founded in the early 1900s, the MoonPie was invented when a salesperson asked a group of coal miners what would be a good snack, and how big should it be? According to MoonPie historian Ronald Dickson, one of the coal miners held up his large hands and framed the full moon rising over the hills. "Bout that big." By the late 1950s, the MoonPie had grown in popularity so much that the bakery did not have the resources available to produce anything else. The phrase "RC Cola and a MoonPie" became well known around the South, as many people enjoyed this delicious, bargain-priced combination.

Today, the Chattanooga Bakery produces over 100 million MoonPies a year. MoonPies are sold in 48 states. Now that's good eating!

MoonPie is a registered trademark of Chattanooga Bakery, Inc.

# Extra Billy's Barbecue

### 5205 W. Broad Street • Richmond, Virginia 23230
### (804) 282-3949

### 1110 Alverser Drive • Midlothian, Virginia 23113
### (804) 379-8727

Lisa Harr is proud to be a fourth generation restaurant guru. "My dad started Extra Billy's and several other restaurants as did my grandfather and great grandfather. It's in the blood," Lisa said. She, her brothers and the rest of their crew are doing what they love to do—barbecue.

Extra Billy's is a landmark around Richmond. The business started out many years ago as a steak restaurant and the menu slowly changed to barbecue. "When dad decided to make the change to barbecue, he did it slow and correctly. He traveled from North Carolina to Texas and learned as much as he could." Lisa says that dedication is why Extra Billy's is so popular.

Four generations of family running restaurants has not been lost on Lisa and her brothers. "We now have a second Extra Billy's. It's located about 30 minutes away. This one is larger, more tables, has an in-house micro brewery and a special mini door for junior customers to enter."

**GREAT EATS:** Extra Billy's serves up their signature pulled pork plates and sandwiches as well as slow-cooked, Virginia-seasoned baby back ribs.

**NEAT THING:** Extra Billy's is named after the Civil War General William Smith. The General served two un-consecutive terms as governor. "Dad was a history buff and liked Extra Billy because he was quite a character."

# Country Mixed Berry Cobbler

*Some fresh hot cobbler with a scoop of vanilla ice cream on the side is a great dessert dish to follow a barbecue dinner.*

2 cups strawberries
2 cups blueberries
2 cups raspberries
2 tablespoons cornstarch
¾ cup sugar
2 tablespoons brown sugar
1½ cups self-rising flour
¼ teaspoon salt

⅓ cup butter, melted
⅓ cup milk
¼ cup apple juice
2 tablespoons butter, melted
Dash nutmeg
Dash cinnamon
Dash brown sugar

First wash all of your berries. Use fresh fruit if possible. Mix berries, cornstarch, sugar, and brown sugar in a large bowl; coat all berries well. Combine the flour, salt, melted butter, milk, and apple juice in another bowl and mix well. Pour your berry mixture into a baking dish and spoon the flour mixture over the top. Combine 2 table-spoons melted butter with a dash each of nutmeg, cinnamon and brown sugar in a small bowl and brush over the top. Bake in a 375° oven for about 25 to 30 minutes or until the topping is golden brown. Serve hot.

# Easy Peach & Blueberry Cobbler

*My mom gave me this recipe. I could not believe how easy it was.*

16 ounces frozen peaches, thawed
½ cup frozen blueberries, thawed

1 box jiffy yellow cake mix
1 (12-ounce) can diet cream soda
1 teaspoon cinnamon

Place peaches and blueberries evenly across the bottom of a glass cake dish. Pour cake mix over the top and very gently pour diet cream soda over the cake mix. Bake uncovered in a 325° to 350° oven for about 30 minutes or until the top is golden brown. Sprinkle with cinnamon just after removing from oven.

# Cherry Cheesecake

*Cheesecake does not get any easier than this.*

2 (8-ounce) packages cream
  cheese, softened
3 eggs, beaten
¾ cup sugar
½ tablespoon vanilla

1 graham cracker pie crust
1 pack chopped nuts
1 pack or can cherry topping or
  pie filling

In a large bowl, combine cream cheese, eggs, sugar, and vanilla; mix with a mixer. Preheat your oven to about 325°. Pour the mixture in the crust and bake for about 25 minutes or until the pie puffs up a bit. Remove from the oven and chill. Spread chopped mixed nuts over the top of the cheesecake and then add the cherry topping. Allow to chill before serving.

# Hot Fruit

*This delicious hot dish from Neilah Hopper is great with your winter barbecue.*

1 can chunk pineapple, drain
  and reserve juice
1 can sliced pears, drain
  and reserve juice
1 can sliced peaches, drain
  and reserve juice
½ bottle cherries (half cut),
  drain and reserve juice

½ cup sugar
¾ cup (3 sticks) margarine
1½ tablespoons cornstarch
1 cup reserved fruit juice
  from drained, canned fruit

Arrange all drained fruit in a baking dish. Mix sugar, margarine, cornstarch and fruit juice. Cook over medium heat until it starts to thicken. Pour over the fruit and chill as long as possible. Bake in a 250° oven for about 30 minutes.

# Pappy's Baked Cider Apples

*This recipe was given to me by Steve L., a barbecue nut from North Carolina. It's simple and tasty.*

Remove cores of 6 good-sized apples. Plug up the bottom of each and cut out V-shape at top. Insert into the hole about 1 tablespoon of Red Hots, 1 tablespoon maple syrup and 1 teaspoon brown sugar. Place the apples in a baking dish and pour about 2½ cups cider around the apples. Bake at 350°, basting occasionally with the hot cider, until tender. When done remove from oven and serve hot in a bowl with ice cream and whipped cream.

# Phillip's Smoked Chocolate Apples

*This recipe from Phillip P. serves two, so just add a few more apples and such for guests.*

**1 huge red apple (I use large
   Red Delicious)**
**1 chocolate bar**
**1 tablespoon caramel syrup**

**1 tablespoon cinnamon**
**1 tablespoon sugar**
**1 tablespoon honey**

Split the apple in half and use a melon baller to scoop out the seeds, leaving a nice pit in the middle of the apple. Next, place the apple on the smoker face down. If you are using indirect heat, cook for about 30 minutes. Next, turn the apples over and fill the pit with pieces of the chocolate and some caramel syrup; leave on the grill (face up) until chocolate has melted. Plate and sprinkle with some cinnamon and sugar and a drizzle of honey. Yum! Yum!

# Homemade Pie Crust

1¼ cups all-purpose flour
1 tablespoon sugar
1 pinch brown sugar
½ teaspoon salt
6 tablespoons butter, room
  temperature

2 tablespoons shortening
3½ cups cold water
½ teaspoon lemon juice

Combine flour, sugar, brown sugar and salt in a bowl; blend well. Add butter and mix. Add shortening and mix. Add water and lemon, and mix. Form dough into a ball and press. Wrap in cling wrap and store in the fridge for an hour or so. Remove, unwrap and place on wax paper. Dust with flour and begin to press and roll the dough from the center out. Place in pan, making sure there are no air bubbles. Remove extra dough from edges, prick bottom with a fork for air holes, and pre-bake at 400° for about 8 to 10 minutes.

## JAKE SAYS —

A dash of cinnamon (or other spices) adds some great flavor to your pie crust. Or just lightly sprinkle it onto the crust before adding the filling.

# Kentucky Bourbon Pecan Pie

*I was born in Kentucky, raised in Tennessee, and I'm growing wiser in Georgia. I have swam in and under oceans, climbed mountains, fought fires, drove a rescue truck and seen a grand slam. But I know that no matter what I do, there are several things in Kentucky that make me feel at home. Basketball, the Derby, Fort Campbell and Kentucky Bourbon. Of course, Lynchburg, Tennessee, makes some pretty good stuff as well.*

**1 unbaked, 8-inch pastry shell**
**4 eggs, beaten**
**1 cup brown sugar**
**¾ cup maple syrup**

**1 tablespoon bourbon**
**3 tablespoons butter, melted**
**1 cup chopped pecans**

Preheat oven to 400° and bake shell for about 5 minutes. Mix eggs, sugar, syrup, bourbon, and butter together and beat well. Remove shell from oven and spread pecans on shell. Slowly pour mixture over pecans and place in oven. Bake for about 30 minutes at 400° and then reduce heat and bake for 45 minutes at 300°. Reduce the oven to 200° and cook for an additional 30 minutes or so. The pie is done when firm in the center and pecans are cooked to a golden brown.

# Arleta's Derby Day Dessert

*We (I can say that because I was born in Kentucky) tend to like our horses in the Bluegrass State. That means we also like the Kentucky Derby. Here is a simple recipe for a semi-traditional Derby Pie. The only difference is that my mom's version does not have any Kentucky Bourbon in the recipe. Submitted by Arleta Whitaker – Mom – Nashville, Tennessee*

**1 stick butter, softened**
**2 eggs, beaten**
**1 cup chocolate chips**
**1 cup sugar**

**1 cup chopped nuts**
**½ cup flour**
**1 teaspoon vanilla flavoring**
**1 prepared pie shell**

Mix all ingredients well, except pie shell. Spoon into pie shell. Bake in 375° oven for about 35 minutes. Let cool in the fridge and top with some whipped topping. Don't tell my mom, but a shot of bourbon makes for some added zest!

# Cherry and Apple Pie

1 can cherry pie filling
4 cups peeled, sliced apples
1 tablespoon maple syrup
1 tablespoon brown sugar
¼ cup all-purpose flour

½ teaspoon ground cinnamon
1 (2-crust) pie pastry, for a
    9-inch pie
1 tablespoon butter or
    margarine, melted

Preheat oven to 400°. In a large mixing bowl, combine cherries and apple slices; add maple syrup and mix. In a small bowl, stir together sugar, flour and cinnamon. Pour over fruit mixture; toss to blend. Let stand 15 minutes. Pour into prepared 9-inch pie pan. Place the top crust over the pie and cut slits. Bake in 400° oven for about 45 to 50 minutes or until crust is golden brown; brush with butter during the last few minutes of baking. Serve warm with a scoop of your favorite ice cream.

# All-American Apple Pie

*This recipe comes from a nice lady we met at the division two NCAA championship football game in Chattanooga in 2002. Her name was Bev and she wrote this down for us. The trick is the crust topping of butter and brown sugar.*

3 pounds (about 7 large) apples
¾ cup granulated sugar
½ teaspoon cinnamon
½ teaspoon freshly grated
    nutmeg
2 to 3 tablespoons cornstarch

¼ teaspoon salt
1 tablespoon fresh lemon juice
2 ready-to-use pie crusts
2 tablespoons unsalted butter,
    melted
1 tablespoon brown sugar

Quarter, core, peel, and slice apples into ¼-inch-thick wedges. Mix with granulated sugar, cinnamon, nutmeg, cornstarch, salt, and lemon juice, and pour into pie crust. Cover with second crust and cut slits in top. Bake in preheated oven at 375° for 1 hour or until top crust is golden brown. Combine butter and brown sugar; brush on top crust before removing from oven. Serve hot!

# Chocolate Ice Box Pie

1 (14-ounce) can sweetened
  condensed milk
2 (1-ounce) squares
  unsweetened chocolate
¼ teaspoon salt

½ cup water
½ teaspoon vanilla extract
1 (9-inch) pie shell, baked
  and cooled
1 cup whipping cream, whipped

Cook first 3 ingredients in top of double boiler over hot water until thick. Add water slowly and let thicken again. Stir in vanilla extract. Pour into pie shell; refrigerate until set. Serve cold with whipped cream on top.

## Deck Chef Tip!

### Crusty Pie Tips

Many great Southern ladies will tell you that a pie is only as good as the crust it comes on. Yes, today I use pre-made crusts purchased in the freezer section of my local store more than I make my own. (I do admit it!) But, in an effort to make things right, here are a few recipes for some great tasting pie crusts. But first, here are some traditional pastry-pie-crust-making tips:

- Do not overwork the dough.
- Keep all ingredients chilled.
- Use chilled butter softened, not melted.
- Roll dough from the center out when making crust.
- Do not double recipe for pie crust and top crust. Instead, make two batches.
- After you work your crust into the pan, chill it for a few minutes.
- Make sure there are no air pockets under the crust.

# Sweetwater Valley Farm

**17988 West Lee Highway • Philadelphia, Tennessee 37846**
**(865) 458-9192 • (877) 862-4332**

On many of my trips up and down Interstate 75, a small sign always caught my attention. The small, bright yellow sign proudly proclaimed, "Cheese." Every trip I would think to myself that on the next trip I would stop by for a look. I finally did, and while this book is dedicated to barbe-cue, a little cheese is not going to hurt any-thing. Of course some of the cheese is smoked.

Sweetwater Valley Farm is located between the towns of Loudon and Philadelphia, Tennessee. The cheese-making facility is in the heart of the dairy-rich Sweetwater Valley in southeast Tennessee. You pull off the interstate, head down a highway, and turn into a real farm with cows walking around. At the top of the drive is a large building with a front porch that opens into a great gift shop and cheese outlet store. The ladies were more than help-ful in telling me all about the process of making cheese. You can watch the cheese being made because the entire back wall of the gift shop is glass. On the other side workers are busy at their craft.

They will also load you up with all kinds of great recipes, let you try a few bites, and make suggestions on what cheese would fit your taste buds. My favorite is the Mountain White Mild Cheddar and the Hickory Smoked White Cheddar. They smoke the cheese for about 14 hours using hickory smoke for a flavor that will knock your socks off! They also make a great cheese loaded with garlic . . . and many more.

# Louise Huskey's Icebox Pie

*This recipe comes from Louise Huskey, a family friend who lives in Wear's Valley, Tennessee. Wear's Valley is located between Sevierville and Townsend on the boundary of Smoky Mountains National Park.*

**2 pie crusts**
**1 can condensed milk**
**1 (8-ounce) pack cream cheese, softened**
**1 (12-ounce) tub whipped topping**

**1 stick butter**
**1 cup chopped pecans**
**7 ounces coconut**
**7 ounces butterscotch syrup**

Bake crust according to the directions on the package, and allow to cool. Mix condensed milk, cream cheese, and whipped topping. Melt butter in a small saucepan and stir in pecans and coconut; cool. Fill both crusts with condensed milk filling mix and top with the butter pecan mix. Spoon on a light topping of butterscotch syrup. Place in the fridge to set.

# Blueberry-Topped Icebox Pie

*Connie Crawford of Nashville, Tennessee, is a great friend of my Mom's who can cook everything from quail to great pies. The quail is a different story, but here is her blueberry-topped pie recipe.*

**2 prepared pie shells (dough or crumb)**
**⅔ cup crushed pecans or more**
**8 ounces whipped topping**

**8 ounces cream cheese, softened**
**1½ cups powdered sugar**
**1 can blueberry pie filling**

If using dough-type pie shells, bake them. Layer the bottom of the pie crust with crushed pecans. In a bowl, mix remaining ingredients, except for the blueberries. Gently pour into the shells. Chill overnight if possible and top with a layer of blueberries. Here is a great tip: spread the blueberries to about ½-inch away from the edge of the pie crust. Serve slices topped with a bit more whipped topping and pecans.

# Easy Graham Cracker Crumb Crust

*Here is a recipe for a very simple crust perfect for icebox-style pies.*

1½ cup finely crushed
  graham cracker crumbs
1 tablespoon granulated sugar

1 tablespoon brown sugar
½ cup melted butter

Crush the crackers into very small pieces. Combine with both sugars. Slowly stir in melted butter until you have a thick, pliable ball. More, or a bit less, butter may be needed. Before the butter begins to re-harden, press the mix into an 8-inch pie shell. Try to make sure the crust is the same thickness all across the pan. Chill in the fridge before adding any filling.

# Helen's Pumpkin Gingersnap Pie

*Mrs. Helen Hoffelt of Nashville, Tennessee, did her best to teach me how to play the piano. I can't say the lesson took, but look at the student she had to work with. I did, however, learn all about her Pumpkin Gingersnap Pie. Now you can, too.*

1½ cups cold milk
1 package instant vanilla
  pudding
8 ounces whipped topping
1 cup ginger snap crumbs
1 cup chopped pecans

½ cup canned pumpkin
  pie filling
½ teaspoon vanilla extract
1 prepared graham cracker
  pie crust

Mix all together and pour in the pie crust. Place in the freezer for at least an hour or so before serving. Top with whipped topping and chopped nuts if desired.

# Nanny's Ice Box Peanut Butter Pie

*This recipe was given to us by a nice lady named "Nanny" who lives in East Tennessee. She says she has been making versions of this pie for as long as she can remember, but now it is easier than ever! We tried it, liked it and then made a few more.*

¼ cup peanut butter, creamy
  or chunky
¼ cup granulated sugar
1 teaspoon vanilla flavoring
4 ounces cream cheese,
  softened
1 (8-ounce) container whipped
  topping

1 (8-inch) pie crust, graham
  cracker or chocolate crumb
½ cup chocolate chips
½ cup peanut butter flavored
  chips

Mix all except the crust, chocolate chips and peanut butter flavored chips. Stir until well mixed and add to pie crust. Melt chocolate chips with a drop or two of oil in the microwave. Do the same with the peanut butter chips. Stir each separately until they are liquid. Take a spoon and drizzle each over the top of the pie; I like to do it like a criss-cross with a very thin bead. Place in freezer and chill until set. Serve semi-frozen.

*If you're ever in Pickens, South Carolina, be sure to stop by Yoder's at Meece Mill. Elise and her family serve up great food, great gifts, and lots of friendship.*

# Triple G Tradin' Post

### 297 County Road 649 • Mentone, Alabama 35984
### (256) 634-8800

Triple G is located high atop Lookout Mountain in Mentone, Alabama. "We call it Triple G because my name is Sonny Gilbreath and I have a son and he has a son. There are three of us." Sonny and his wife Frances decided to go into the antique business a while back after the business he worked for moved, was bought and moved again. "I just thought it was too long of a drive, and we decided to do this." The building was hand-built by Sonny, Frances, friends and family. "It took about two years."

Triple G actually started as a full antique business. One day Frances Gilbreath decided to start serving cakes, pies and coffee to customers. Now the restaurant is the main attraction with the antique shop opened off to the side. The Triple G menu offers great barbecue, big ol' char grilled burgers, lots of sides and desserts.

**NEAT THING:** Take a minute to play checkers on the front porch if the table is open. "I would like to do a checkers tournament some-day," Sonny said.

# Triple G's Peanut Butter Pie

*When you write a weekly food column, write cookbooks and hang out with chef-type folk you tend to eat a bunch. Sometimes all you need is a nice piece of pie. When I visited Triple G's Trading Post and BBQ on Lookout Mountain in Mentone, Alabama, it was very early in the morning and I had already eaten barbecue twice that day. During our conversation, Sonny and Frances offered up something different. Several slices of different kinds of pie. Here is Frances' recipe for possibly the best peanut butter pie in the South.*

| | |
|---|---|
| 4 ounces cream cheese, room temperature | 8 ounces whipped topping |
| 1 cup powdered sugar | ¾ cup peanut butter |
| | 9-inch graham cracker pie crust |

Whip cream cheese until fluffy. Add powdered sugar, and mix well. Fold in whipped topping and peanut butter; blend well. Spoon mixture into crust and smooth the top as flat as possible. Place in fridge while making topping.

**CHOCOLATE GLAZE TOPPING:**

| | |
|---|---|
| 2 ounces chocolate chips | 1 teaspoon corn syrup |
| ¼ cup whipping cream, whipped | |

In a small saucepan, over low heat, melt chocolate chips. Stir in whipped cream and corn syrup. Stir until smooth then remove from heat. Gently glaze over the pie. Place in fridge and chill for at least two hours before serving.

# How to Make Whipped Cream

*Believe it or not, real whipped cream does not only come in those plastic tubs in the cooler section of the grocery store. Those tubs are great in a pinch, but if you get a chance, making whipped cream is fairly simple. Here is the secret, use heavy cream and confectioners' sugar instead of whipping cream and granulated sugar. My mom says add a bit of vanilla for extra flavor.*

Pour ½ pint heavy cream in a bowl; add a few drops of vanilla flavoring. Begin whipping the cream with an electric mixer for about a minute. Measure a big tablespoon of confectioners' sugar. Add in half the sugar and whip for about 30 seconds. Add the rest of the sugar and continue to whip until peaks appear. Be careful not to over whip; you'll end up making a bowl of butter.

# Jamie's Easy Banana Pudding

*Jamie believes in easy-to-make, flavorful dishes. She also believes that any good cookout requires some good banana pudding. Yes, you can make great banana pudding with instant pudding. The trick is to use lots of bananas and homemade whipped cream.*

| | |
|---|---|
| **2 ripe bananas** | **Lots of vanilla wafers** |
| **2 boxes instant vanilla pudding** | **Large carton of whipping cream** |
| **1 tablespoon vanilla flavoring** | **Sugar as required to whip cream** |

When you make vanilla pudding, follow Jamie's banana pudding philosophy. Big bowls with lots of wafers and fresh whipped cream. And kids get extra vanilla wafers on the side for dipping.

What would any good cookout be without a bowl of 'nanner pudding? According to the Nabisco Company, the modern version of banana pudding comes from a recipe printed on the side of a box of Nabisco Nilla Wafers many years ago. Try layering banana pudding in mason jars or wine glasses. Or serve it in a waffle-style ice cream cone.

# No-Egg Butter-Pecan Ice Cream

*If making a custard-based ice cream scares you, then here is a very easy recipe for great No-Egg Butter-Pecan Ice Cream.*

1 cup finely chopped pecans
2 tablespoons butter
1 teaspoon brown sugar
2½ cups heavy cream

¾ cup sugar
2 tablespoons vanilla extract
2 cups cold milk

In a skillet, brown pecans in butter; remove from heat and add brown sugar. Stir to ensure the pecans are well and evenly coated. Mix pecans with remaining ingredients and then follow the directions on your ice cream maker. Serve ice cold!

# Kid's Easy Ice Cream Cake

*This is a great dessert that the kids can help you with. It requires little or no knowledge of a kitchen or oven. THAT'S EASY! All you have to do is open a few boxes, un-wrap a few things, chill, serve and eat!*

1 box ice cream sandwiches
1 carton of your favorite ice
   cream

1 bottle hard shell chocolate
1 container whipped cream
2 chocolate candy bars

Arrange as many ice cream sandwiches as will fit on the bottom of a glass cake dish. Let your ice cream soften a bit and spread over the ice cream sandwiches. Squirt the whole bottle of hard shell topping over the ice cream. Place in the freezer and freeze. Before serving, cover with whipped cream and shave the candy bars over the top.

# Easy Chocolate Ice Cream

*I love chocolate chip ice cream. This recipe makes chocolate ice cream or chocolate chip ice cream. Just vary the time when you add the chocolate chips. For a deeper chocolate taste, just toss in some more chocolate chips.*

**1 quart half-and-half**
**1¼ cups (or 14-ounce can)**
  **condensed milk**

**2½ teaspoons vanilla extract**
**1 cup semi-sweet chocolate chips**

Beat half-and-half, condensed milk and vanilla extract in large mixer bowl until combined. Add to your ice cream maker and follow the directions for making ice cream. If you want chocolate ice cream, add the chocolate chips in with the other ingredients. If you want chocolate chip ice cream, add the chocolate chips towards the end of the freezing process.

**Variation for Vanilla Ice Cream:** Follow the directions above but forget the chips. Instead, try adding some blueberries, strawberries or maybe even some bananas.

I'm told that ice cream probably originated in China. Commercial ice cream manufacturing in the United States began around the mid 1800s. These early ice cream producers made ice cream the same way we do at home, just on a larger scale. They placed the ingredients in a large metal container and surrounded it with a mixture of ice and salt; the canister was rotated until the creamy mixture was thick and smooth. BRING ME A SPOON! Today, many commercial ice cream recipes are, in fact, a form of frozen custard.

# Deck Chef Tip!

## Safely Making Ice Cream

Nothing makes a great barbecue cookout like some home-made ice cream. Many of us remember making sure the ice and salt mixture was just right so the canister kept turning. I remember the hand-crank ice cream maker at my grandparents' house, and the sore arms my brothers and I got turning the crank.

We all love homemade ice cream as a dessert for cook-outs. But if the recipe you're using contains raw eggs, you may need to update it. Raw eggs may contain salmonella bacteria. Who knows, maybe that stomach ache you had was not from eating hot potato salad that sat out in the sun, but from the creamy, homemade ice cream you ate. While most people with salmonella poisoning suffer only from mild discomfort, infants, children, seniors and those with lowered immune systems could get a lot sicker . . . and worse.

So what do you do? Look for recipes that require no raw eggs, or commercial mixes that use gelatin instead. You can also use pasteurized egg substitutes instead. These are sold in many grocery stores. They often come in small containers that look like milk cartons.

If your recipe does call for eggs and milk, you might want to precook it. Place your milk and beaten eggs in a saucepan and cook on low to medium heat. Be sure to stir constantly. Congratulations, you just made a cooked custard ice cream!

# Neva Owens

### Barbecue Diva

I can't talk about barbecue without mentioning my good friend Neva Owens. Better known as Neva the Barbecue Diva, she LIVES barbecue. Neva was the owner of Owens Bar-B-Que, which was located in an amazing building built in the winter of 1938 in Rome, Georgia. "It has been here for a long time and is full of food history," Neva said. "The lady that owned the house sold meals for twenty-five cents to the workers building the road."

"I love barbecue, I love to cook, and most of all, I love my customers and this building," Neva says. But, as all things must change, Neva is moving along the culinary path. "I am going to do a few things I have always wanted to do. Maybe culinary school, bartending school, classes in management, and just getting creative with my cooking."

I've learned many barbecue secrets from Neva who considers herself "a barbecue purest." Her barbecue advice is simple, but best taken to heart.

"Always barbecue for friends and family. Use fresh ingredients and take your time," said Neva. "The most important part of barbecue is to take things slow and easy. The best part of that is it gives you time to have good conversation with your friends."

# Picnic Jam Cookies

*Wanda S. over in North Carolina told me her 4th of July picnics would not be complete unless these cookies were on the table. She started baking them for Christmas, but her family likes them so much that she makes them during the summer as well.*

**1½ cups all-purpose flour**
**1 teaspoon baking powder**
**½ teaspoon cinnamon**
**¼ teaspoon cloves**
**½ teaspoon salt**
**2 tablespoons vegetable**
  **shortening**

**¼ cup applesauce**
**½ cup confectioners' sugar**
**1 whole egg, or ¼ cup**
  **egg substitute**
**½ teaspoon vanilla extract**
**½ cup strawberry preserves**
**Confectioners' sugar**

Preheat oven to 400°. In a large bowl, mix flour, baking powder, cinnamon, cloves, and salt. In a separate bowl, mix vegetable shortening and applesauce. Add sugar, egg and vanilla.

Add flour mixture to applesauce mixture. Blend until smooth (mixture will be pretty stiff).

Using flour-coated hands, roll

## JAKE SAYS —

Cookies make a perfect easy-to-take-along dessert for any outdoor event.

teaspoons of dough into balls. Place on well greased cookie sheet. Press your thumb into center to make a small dent. Fill with ½ teaspoon of strawberry preserves. Bake the cookies for about 15 minutes or until light golden brown. Remove from oven and allow cookies to cool. Then sprinkle a bit confectioners' sugar over each cookie

# Sugar Cookie Tree

*My buddy Marci brought a huge cookie, stacked in layers and shaped like a Christmas tree to the office one day. Ever since then, I knew she was cool. Here is Marci's Sugar Cookie Tree recipe.*

| | |
|---|---|
| 1 cup shortening | ¼ teaspoon baking soda |
| 2 cups sugar | ½ teaspoon salt |
| 3 eggs | 4 cups flour |
| ¼ cup milk | 2 teaspoons almond flavoring |
| 1 teaspoon baking powder | |

Cream shortening and sugar; add eggs, and mix until creamy. Add milk, dry ingredients and almond flavoring. It will be very hard to mix, so use your hands and mix well. I prefer to use bread dough hooks to mix the dough. They work just as well.

Store in the refrigerator for about 1 hour. Roll out the dough on a floured board. Cut out star patterns in the dough using stars of at least 6 different sizes. (Star cookie cutters can be found in specialty stores.) Before cooking, cut a hole in the center of each star for a wooden dowel. This dowel holds the tree in place.

After stars are cut, round cookies need to be cut (juice glass size). Except for the top couple of layers, those round cookies need to be smaller than the stars. A center hole needs to be placed in each of these. The round cookies will be used to layer between each star when making the tree. You will need 2 cookies of each size for each tree.

Bake the cookies at 350° until edges are brown.

## ICING FOR THE TREE:

| | |
|---|---|
| 4 tablespoons (¼ cup) butter, softened | 4 tablespoons plus 2 teaspoons almond flavoring |
| 2 cups powdered sugar | 2 teaspoons white corn syrup |
| 3 tablespoons milk | Green food coloring, as desired |

Mix until smooth. Cover bowl when not in use so the icing does not harden before you are done.

## TO ASSEMBLE TREE:

Tree can be assembled two different ways. This first way is using the dowel. Take the largest stars and ice them and the round cookies to go between them. Place dowel on the surface that you want the tree

*(continued)*

*(Sugar Cookie Tree continued)*

to stand on. Slide iced star down the dowel. Then slide round cookie on to it. Take second star and rotate it so that the points of the star point in different directions than the first, then slide it down the dowel. Continue this process until all cookies are used. The largest stars go on the bottom working your way to the smallest stars at the top.

Another way to assemble the tree is without the dowel. Simply layer the tree as you did in the above manner, placing each cookie on top of the other. The icing will hold the tree together when it starts to harden.

After the tree is assembled, decorate the tree. This can be done with powdered sugar sprinkled on the branches to simulate snow, or with gumdrops on the branches. You can also mix up more icing without the green food coloring and drizzle it over the branches to simulate snow and ice hanging from the tree.

# Black Walnut Cookies

*Walnuts make for great cookies. Here is a simple and classic recipe for some of the best cookies you'll ever bake.*

**2 cups brown sugar**
**4 eggs, well beaten**
**½ cup flour**

**½ teaspoon salt**
**½ teaspoon baking powder**
**2 cups chopped walnuts**

Mix brown sugar, eggs, flour, salt, and baking powder. Stir in nuts. Drop by teaspoonfuls onto a greased baking sheet, and bake about 12 minutes at 350°.

# The Perfect S'more!

*Many people have great memories of church camp, Boy Scouts, Girl Scouts or family outings where this warm, drippy combination of graham crackers, chocolate and a toasted marshmallow was made over an open fire while laughter filled the air.*

Simply place a marshmallow on a stick, heat it up over a fire, slap it on a graham cracker and add a piece of chocolate bar. Just as the chocolate melts, put another graham cracker on top. And yes, in case you have not tried them, a barbecue buddy introduced me to s'mores made with chocolate chip cookies, sugar cookies and even s'mores dipped fondue-style! YUM!! For added flavor some people add sliced bananas, apples, berries and more!

# Grilled Apple Biscuits

**2 cans biscuits**
**½ cup apple sauce**
**½ cup peeled and finely chopped apples**
**½ cup brown sugar**
**½ cup melted butter**
**¼ cup chopped pecans**

Mix all ingredients, including biscuits, in a bowl. Make sure each biscuit gets coated well. Place all into a well greased cake or bread pan and bake in a preheated 400° covered grill for about 25 minutes. Of course you can do this in the oven as well.

# Jane's Cheesy Fudge

*Jane from East Tennessee is a great lady who stopped by our old hot sauce shop several times. During one of the visits, she dropped off this recipe for Cheesy Fudge.*

**1 pound (4 sticks) butter**
**1 pound Velveeta**
**4 pounds confectioners' sugar**
**1 cup cocoa**
**1 tablespoon vanilla**
**½ cup chopped nuts**

Melt the first two ingredients together in a double boiler. Sift together the sugar and cocoa. Combine both mixtures thoroughly with vanilla and chopped nuts. Pour into buttered pans.

# Barbecue Jargon

**Ever been watching a cooking show on TV,** the host says something, and you have no idea what the heck he/she is talking about? When ya get to barbecuing real good, you'll find yourself chatting up with other chef types and pit master folk. You don't want to be lacking in the way of the cooking terms. So here is a list of basic, need-to-know cooking terms with some barbecue jargon basted on.

**aerate** Aerate is sort of like sifting. You pass your ingredients through a mesh screen to bust up large chunks and make it airy so it will be lighter and fluffy.

**au jus** Au jus is the drippings or juice from cooked meat in the bottom of the pan. Au jus is the juice before adding stuff like flour and spices to make gravy.

**baby back ribs** Baby back ribs are ribs that have extra fat and cartilage removed by the butcher or meat packer. These make for easy to handle, tender ribs that have little waste.

**bake** This is easy. To cook in the oven is to bake. Food is cooked slowly with constant heat. You can bake in an oven, Dutch oven, covered grill or even a smoker.

**Barbecue, BBQ, bar-be-cue, bar-b-que, barbeque** Even though the people who package uncovered charcoal grills and such would have you think differently, barbecuing is simply a method of cooking that uses low heat, smoke, long cooking times and seasonings. This causes the connective tissue and fats to break down in the meat being cooked. This combines with the smoky flavor of wood, giving barbecue its distinctive taste.

**baste** When you baste meat, you just brush, mop or spoon sauces or juices over meat while cooking. This adds flavor and to helps to prevent the meat from drying out.

**batter** A batter is a mixture of flour, fat or oil, spices and liquid that is thin enough that you can dip your food to be cooked in it. A batter is different from dough because dough will hold its shape for a short period of time while a batter is more liquid-like. Simply put, batters look like pancake mix and dough looks like canned biscuits.

**beat** Beating means you smooth a mix by whipping or stirring it with a spoon, fork, wire whisk or electric mixer.

**blackened** Blackened dishes simply are versions of a popular Cajun-style cooking method. Highly seasoned foods are cooked over high heat in a super-heated heavy skillet until the spices and outer layer of meat are charred. The inside remains moist and full of flavor.

**blanch** To boil briefly to loosen the skin of a fruit or a vegetable. After 30 seconds in boiling water, the fruit or vegetable should be plunged into ice water to stop further cooking. Jamie does great veggies such as green beans using the blanching method.

**Boston Butt** A Boston Butt is actually a cut of shoulder. I'm told the name comes from the way the packing company that coined the term packed the meat. The finished cuts were packed in large containers called "butts."

**braise** A cooking technique that requires browning meat in oil or other fat and then cooking slowly in liquid. The effect of braising is to tenderize the meat. Sometimes you can braise with additional seasonings to boost flavor.

**breaded** Catfish never tasted so good! Breaded coatings are almost a dry version of a batter. When you bread, you coat the food with crumbs or flour. Most often the meat is first dipped in a liquid such as milk or egg whites. Breading mixes can be seasoned with dashes of salt, pepper and even red pepper.

**broil** When you broil foods, you cook food directly under or over a heat source. In the kitchen you can broil in the oven. On the grill searing is very close to broiling.

**broth or stock** A broth or stock is a flavorful liquid made by cooking meat, seafood, or vegetables, often with herbs, in liquid, usually water. Stocks are perfect starters or ingredients in other dishes.

**browning** Browning is a quick sautéing, pan/oven broiling, or grilling method

done either at the beginning or end of meal preparation, often to enhance flavor, texture, or eye appeal. A great example of browning is when I brown the outside edges of some fresh grouper in a skillet with a bit of olive oil and then bake the fish in the oven to finish.

**Bundt pan** A Bundt pan is the generic name for any tube-shaped baking pan.

*You'll find this neat, little smoker behind King's, a small restaurant combination grocery store that offers the best barbecue in the Charleston, Tennessee area.*

**butterfly** When you butterfly a steak, chicken breast, chop or whatever, you cut the food down the center without cutting all the way through, and then spread apart. Think about butterfly steaks or stuffed pork chops.

**caramelization** Browning sugar over a flame, with or without the addition of some water to aid the process. You can caramelize in an oven or even get a cool little blow torch to do the job.

**chiffon** Chiffon is often a pie filling that is made light and fluffy by using stabilized gelatin and beaten egg whites.

**chipotle** You've tasted in sauces at many restaurants but did you ever know what it was? Chipotle flavoring is the deep taste of smoked jalapeño peppers.

**clarify** When you clarify a liquid, you remove impurities by heating the liquid, then straining or skimming it. Stocks are often clarified.

**core** Sometimes you just can't eat the whole thing. When you core, you remove the inedible center of fruits such as pineapples.

**cream** The reason you cream something is to trap tiny air bubbles inside the mix. This is the secret to fluffy biscuits, cookies and cakes. When you cream, you beat vegetable shortening, butter, or margarine, with or without sugar, until light and fluffy.

**crimp** Crimping is done to create a decorative edge on a pie crust, Calzone or homemade stuffed barbecue pocket. Not only is it cool to look at, it also seals the edges together.

**custard** Custard is a mixture of beaten egg, milk, and other ingredients such as sweet flavorings. Then the mix is cooked with low, gentle heat, often in a water bath or double boiler. As pie filling, the custard is frequently cooked and chilled before being layered into a pre-baked crust.

**dash** How many times have you heard a dash of this or a dash of that? A dash is approximately equal to $1/16$ teaspoon. It can also depend on how big your fingers are when you pick up a dash of something.

**deep-fry**  Deep Fried Turkey! Deep-frying is different from skillet-frying because you completely submerge the food in seasoned hot oil.

**devilized**  Devil, or devilized, means that spicy ingredients such as cayenne pepper or hot sauce has been added to a food.  An example would, of course, be deviled eggs.

**direct heat**  A cooking method that allows heat to meet food directly, such as grilling, broiling, or toasting.

**dipping sauce**  A dipping sauce is a thick sauce used for dipping foods.  Hey, that's called dip!

**dough**  A dough is a combination of ingredients including flour, water or milk, and, sometimes a leavener, producing a firm but workable mixture for making baked goods.  A dough holds its shape longer than a batter.  Like I stated before, think of canned biscuits.

**drizzle**  When you drizzle, you pour a liquid such as a sweet glaze or melted butter in a slow, light trickle over food.  Drizzles are often used to apply icing to pastries, cakes and such.

**dust**  Who knew funnel cakes at the county fair were so high class?  Dusting a food means you sprinkle the food lightly with spices, sugar, or flour for a light coating.

**egg wash**  An egg wash is a mixture of beaten eggs with either milk or water.  Used to coat cookies, egg rolls and other baked goods to give them a shine when baked.

**emulsify**  A mixture of liquids, one being a fat or oil and the other being water-based so that tiny globules of one are suspended in the other.  This may involve the use of stabilizers, such as egg or mustard.  Emulsions can be temporary or permanent.

**fillet**  Fillet is simple.  To fillet means to remove the bones from meat or fish for cooking.

**finishing sauce**  A barbecue sauce used towards the end of the cooking process.  It can also be used as a table sauce.

**flambé**  Where is the fire?  When you flambé, you ignite a sauce or other liquid that contains an alcohol so that it flames.  This process produces a quick flame which adds to the final flavoring.  It is also cool to watch.  Be careful, this method can be dangerous.

**fold**  Folding is just mixing lightly with a spoon to keep as much air in the mixture as possible.

**frizzled** Frizzled meats are thin slices of meat cooked in hot oil until crisp and slightly curly.

**garnish** A garnish is a decorative piece of edible ingredient such as parsley, lemon wedges, croutons, or chocolate curls placed as a finishing touch to dishes or drinks.

**grate** When you grate, you shred or cut down a food into fine pieces by rubbing it against a rough surface.

**grill** Grilling is cooking over a heat source such as gas, charcoal and wood.

**headspace** Nope, not the empty-space in your cousin's head . . . but close! Head-space is the air pocket left in home-canned goods.

**jerk or Jamaican jerk seasoning** Jerk seasoning is a dry mixture of spices such as chilies, thyme, garlic, onions, cinnamon or cloves used to season meats such as chicken or pork.

**julienne** Julienne means to cut into long, thin strips. Now you know why they call them Julienne fries!

**knead** Kneading means you work a dough mixture with the heels of your hands in a pressing and folding motion until it becomes smooth and elastic.

**larding** Larding is a way to add some moisture and flavor to tougher cuts of meat by inserting strips of fat into it, so that the braised meat stays moist and juicy.

**loin** A loin is a cut of meat that typically comes from the back of the animal.

**marinade**  A marinade is a liquid seasoning made from vinegar or wine combined with spices and herbs.  Marinades often include a citrus juice.  Delicate meats such as fish and poultry can be marinated in yogurt.

**medallion**  A medallion cut of meat is a small round or oval bit of meat.

**mince**  Minced means the meat, or other food, is chopped into tiny, irregular pieces.

**moisten**  A wet rub is a great example of a moistened food.  To moisten means that enough liquid is added to dry ingredients to dampen but not soak them.

**mop sauce**  A mop sauce is a barbecue sauce that is applied with a mop-style basting brush.

**pan broil**  When you pan broil, you cook a food in a skillet without added fat, removing any fat as it accumulates.  This is a great way to jump start a pot roast.

**pipe**  Pipe is often used with desserts.  It means to force a soft food through a bag with a pastry nozzle.

**pit**  When you pit, you use a sharp knife to take out the center stone or seed of a fruit, such as a peach or a mango.

**Oh... the other pit**  A pit is a hole in the ground for cooking meats.  A pit is also a brick, earthen or metal oven that uses wood, gas, charcoal or indirect heat for cooking.

**purée**  This means to mash or sieve food into a thick liquid.  Put a tomato, an onion, a clove of garlic and a dash of olive oil in a blender and hit the button until you get a thick juice.

**reduce**  When you reduce a liquid, you cook liquids down so that some of the water evaporates.  This thickens a liquid without adding something such as flour.

**roasting**  In general, roasted means to cook a food uncovered in the oven or covered grill.

**roux**  A cooked paste usually made from flour and butter used to thicken sauces.

**rub**  A rub is a mixture of dry spices that is rubbed on food before cooking.  You can consider a rub as a dry marinade.

**sauté**  To cook food quickly in a small amount of oil in a skillet or sauté pan over direct heat.

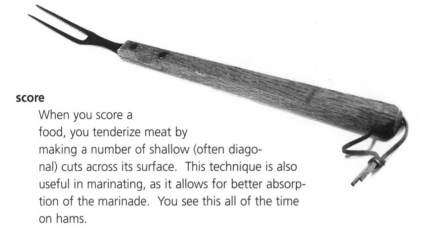

**score**
>When you score a food, you tenderize meat by making a number of shallow (often diagonal) cuts across its surface. This technique is also useful in marinating, as it allows for better absorption of the marinade. You see this all of the time on hams.

**sear**  Searing is cooking over high heat. This seals in a meat's juices by cooking it quickly. Used when cooking tender, thinner cuts of meat.

**shred**  When you shred, you cut or tear the food, or old bank statements, into long narrow strips, either by hand or by using a grater or food processor.

**sift**  Sifting is done to remove large lumps from a dry ingredient such as flour or confectioners' sugar by passing it through a fine mesh. This process also incorporates air into the ingredients, making them lighter.

**simmer**  Cooking food in a liquid at a low enough temperature that small bubbles begin to break the surface.

**steam**  Steamed foods are cooked over boiling water in a covered pan. This method keeps foods' shape, texture, and nutritional value intact better than methods such as boiling.

**steep**  Tea is an easy example of the steep process. It means to soak dry ingredients such as tea leaves, ground coffee, herbs, spices, etc., in a liquid until the flavor is infused into the liquid.

**stewing**  Stewing is browning small pieces of meat, poultry, or fish, then simmering them with vegetables or other ingredients in enough liquid to cover them, usually in a closed pot on the stove, in the oven, or with a slow cooker.

**stir-fry**  The fast frying of small pieces of meat and vegetables over very high heat with continual and rapid stirring.

**truss**  When you truss in cooking, you use string, skewers, or pins to hold together a food to maintain its shape while it cooks.  A truss is often used to hold chicken legs closed when cooking.  A truss can be used on many foods to hold them together during the cooking process.

**unleavened**  Baked goods that contain no agents to give them volume, such as baking powder, baking soda, or yeast, are called unleavened.  During the Civil War, both sides made crackers, or hard tack, from flour, water, salt and a few other ingredients if they were available.

**vinaigrette**  A vinaigrette sauce is a general term referring to any sauce made with vinegar, oil, and seasonings.

**whip**  When you whip, you incorporate air into ingredients such as cream or egg whites by beating until light and fluffy; also refers to the utensil used for this action.

**zest**  The thin, brightly colored outer part of the rind of citrus fruits.  It contains volatile oils, used as a flavoring.

# ON A FINAL NOTE:

Most nights around the grill you can catch me in a baseball jersey and shorts. But sometimes the white coat gets rolled out. A special thanks to all of the places that invite me to come and teach others how to enjoy cooking from a different point of view. You're guaranteed to have fun, hear some stories, trivia and a few recipes and cooking tips tossed. NASCAR talk is always welcome.

Thanks to Heide at Mia Cucina, Nick and the Chattanooga Market, Alan and his love for the Yankees, Wally, J.R., Chip, Anne, my buddy Neva and of course Stan at *The Catoosa County News* and John at Chattanoogan.com.

"Now Let's Get Cooking!"

*I need a few extra hands when doing cooking demos and classes. Here, Marcy and Robin take the time to help me look good during a barbecue class at Mia Cucina in Chattanooga, Tennessee.*

# Index

# Recipe Index

Look for **Smoke in the Mountains Cookbook** in kitchen specialty stores, gift shops, bookstores, or order direct . . .

- Visit us on the web at **www.quailridge.com** and **www.thedeckchef.com.** While you're there check out the free recipes, discount offers, other great books, and so much more.

**JAKE SAYS —**
*Smoke in the Mountains Cookbook makes a great gift!*

- Give us a call at **1-800-343-1583** to order with any major credit card.

- Mail the order form below with your check or money order to **Quail Ridge Press, P. O. Box 123, Brandon, Mississippi 39043.**

- Or fax the order form below with your credit card information to **1-800-864-1082.**

Request a **FREE CATALOG** of all Quail Ridge Press cookbooks by calling **1-800-343-1583.**

# Order Form

**Clip and Send to:  QUAIL RIDGE PRESS • P. O. Box 123 • Brandon, MS  39043**

❏ Check or money order enclosed
Charge to:  ❏ Visa  ❏ MasterCard  ❏ American Express  ❏ Discover

Card # _____  Expiration Date _____

Signature _____  Email Address _____

Name _____  Phone # _____

Address _____

City/State/Zip _____

|  | Quantity | Price | Cost |
|---|---|---|---|
| *Smoke in the Mountains Cookbook* | _____ | @ $16.95 ea. = | _____ |
| 7% Tax for Mississippi residents | | | _____ |
| Postage ($4.00 any number of books) | | | + 4.00 |
| Total | | | _____ |